A Child in the
Principal's
Office

Dedicated to
Nate and Sylvia, for letting me be a child once;
and to
Erica and Maya, for letting me be immature forever.

A Child in the Principal's Office

Laughing and Learning in the Schoolhouse

Richard Lodish

CORWIN PRESS, INC.
A Sage Publications Company
Thousand Oaks, California

For information address:

Corwin Press, Inc.
A Sage Publications Company
2455 Teller Road
Thousand Oaks, California 91320
email: order@corwin.sagepub.com

SAGE Publications Ltd.
6 Bonhill Street
London EC2A 4PU
United Kingdom

SAGE Publications India Pvt. Ltd.
M-32 Market
Greater Kailash I
New Delhi 110 048 India

Printed in the United States of America

Library of Congress Cataloging-in-Publication Data

Lodish, Richard.
    A child in the principal's office : laughing and learning in the
schoolhouse / Richard Lodish.
        p. cm.
    Includes bibliographical references.
    ISBN 0-8039-6381-5 (cloth). — ISBN 0-8039-6382-3 (pbk.)
    1. Lodish, Richard. 2. School principals—United States—
Biography. 3. Sidwell Friends School (Washington, D.C.)
4. Education—United States—Anecdotes.   I. Title.
LA2317.L78A3   1995
371.2'012'092—dc20
    [B]   95-21432

This book is printed on acid-free paper.

    99 00 01 02 03 04 05 10 9 8 7 6 5 4 3

Cover and interior artwork by Di Stovall

Corwin Press Production Editor: S. Marlene Head

Contents

December

January

February

March

April

May

June

July

August

Foreword

Educator Alfred North Whitehead[1] once warned of what he called "'inert ideas'. . . ideas that are merely received into the mind without being utilized or tested, or thrown into fresh combinations. . . . Education has been radically infected with inert ideas."

Anyone who reads Richard Lodish's *A Child in the Principal's Office* will be exposed to one of the leading anti-inert-idea figures in American education. Rich Lodish thinks that there is no more serious calling than education, that it must have relevance to our lives, and that an essential way to achieve relevance is to make it fun. The apt subtitle of this delicious book is *Laughing and Learning in the Schoolhouse*.

Two disclaimers up front. One, Rich Lodish is the principal of the Sidwell Friends Lower School, located on the outskirts of Washington, DC. This Quaker institution isn't your typical American school. Its students include sons and daughters of famous politicians, newspaper publishers, corporate chief executive officers, and the president of the United States. But it is a school that thrives on diversity, and in Rich Lodish's lower school (Grades pre-kindergarten through 4) the school takes its task—but not itself—very seriously.

Second, our three children have spent a combined 12 years at the Sidwell Friends Lower School. Our 14-year-old, Jeffrey, is an alumnus of the lower school, while 8-year-old Benjamin is in the third grade and 6-year-old Lauren is a first grader. As parents, our good-experience batting average puts Cal Ripken's to shame. Since we don't have any more potential applicants to the school, we feel no conflict of interest in praising its principal's literary endeavor.

Actually, our best sources on Rich Lodish are three people we know who have had intimate exposure to him: our three kids. Jeffrey is the 6-year-old in the book who once (affectionately, we trust) told his principal that he was weird. Rich Lodish, using this as an opening to extol diversity, explained to him how most of us have weird characteristics. Jeffrey still thinks Mr. Lodish is weird but now considers it pretty much a compliment.

Lauren notes that he "wears ties sometimes . . . and he is supposed to be serious but he is funny." Benjamin says, without hesitation, "He is an awesome principal." Why? "He just is. I don't know why."

One reason even Benjamin might cite, upon reflection, is the irrepressible Lodish humor—of mixed quality, but omnipresent. While his father was reading this book on a grueling 19-hour train ride from Beijing to Shanghai, Benjamin asked him why he was laughing. It was the story about the mother who let her child out at school, looked away, and then looked back, eyes closed, lips puckered, to say "Bye-bye sweetie" to . . . Mr. Lodish. The rest of the train ride went faster as Benjamin told and retold that story, laughing uproariously each time.

Some 200 years ago, in a poem titled "The Schoolboy," William Blake observed of children in school:

But to go to school in a summer morn,
Oh, it drives all joy away!
Under a cruel eye outworn,
The little ones spend the day
In sighing and dismay.

Many children today would be similarly affected; not those who go to school under Rich Lodish, however. He realizes there are more than a few people who get As in school and then flunk everyday living. The Lodish philosophy, as he explains it, is "If we show children the lighter side of life as a child, they're more likely to grow up as fun-loving people."

If that is true—and we strongly suspect it is—Sidwell Friends is turning out scores of would-be Lettermans and Lenos. This book is an encyclopedia of anecdotes, and it only describes the tip of the iceberg. Fun and humor are staples of the Lodish school of learning.

The atmosphere at this very special school clearly is set by the principal, whether at the annual Halloween parade, on a fishing trip with kids, during a home visit to read a youngster a bedtime story, or in the course of his daily rounds. To be humorless at the Sidwell Friends Lower School is like being a pair of brown shoes at a formal affair.

But the Lodish humor has a decided purpose—to make learning easier and more appealing. It's part of what he calls the "need to provide students with the academic tools and the moral centeredness to be critical thinkers, respectful questioners, and valued community members."

Community and community responsibility are deeply ingrained at a very early age. "The more I hear of the decline in communal spirit within our neighborhoods," Principal Lodish writes, "the more I've come to believe that schools need to provide an alternative structure for engendering this sense of community, not only for our students and teachers, but also for our parents." He goes on to suggest that "without a strong, coherent community, a school will remain at best no more than an adequate place for teaching and learning. With a sense of community, it can become an environment in which caring, respect, and kindness radiate throughout."

As a parent, one invariably is drawn into this community at Sidwell Friends. For a reasonably high-powered group, the lack of prima donnas or arrogant know-it-alls is amazing. With its emphasis on caring camaraderie, and with more than a dash of wit and whimsy tossed in, arrogant prima donnas would be truly offensive. But the Lodish concept of community extends beyond narrow confines. At a very early age, Sidwell Friends youngsters not only learn about but spend time with the less fortunate: making sandwiches for the underprivileged at Martha's Table or visiting with senior citizens. There is little air of noblesse oblige; it is simply in the Quaker spirit, even if only 6% of the kids are Quakers.

Other than humor and commitment, if this book reveals any secret as to how Rich Lodish runs one of the truly great elementary schools in the country, it's his approach to teaching and teachers. Like a top-notch CEO or a great basketball coach, this principal painstakingly searches for the best talent and then lets them do their thing. It's almost unheard-of to hear Rich Lodish second-guess a teacher.

"When teachers are given the freedom to try new ideas and to take risks," Lodish writes, "students also feel free to take risks, to learn from mistakes, and to venture into new areas of learning." After one difficult year, Rich Lodish assigned our oldest child to a teacher who was getting along in years, and who we thought might be too brittle for this task. As we quickly learned, however, she was about as brittle as cast iron; Jeffrey thrived under her constant supportive encouragement and occasional firm exhortations. In a combined dozen years at Sidwell, our kids have never had a bad teacher.

A thought in passing: When the Bob Doles and Bill Clintons focus again on the way Hollywood and television affect our popular culture, they should take a look at how teachers are portrayed. "I touch the future," the late Christa McAuliffe declared at an August 1985 rally in Landover, Maryland. "I teach." This truth isn't very ingrained in most popular culture today, and that's a shame. But it is pervasive throughout this book. (Lodish frequently incorporates popular culture into his writing and "principaling"—quoting from movies, television shows, and well-known songs from the '50s and '60s.) If we had lots more Rich Lodishes, we'd have lots fewer worries about American education.

This unusual principal doesn't micromanage, but he does create the environment. The tone for teaching at Sidwell Friends is child centered, maintaining enough flexibility to meet as many unique needs of as many children as possible. The vast majority of these 5- to 10-year-olds flourish in this environment.

It's hard to find anything to criticize about this splendid book (other than a few bad jokes). This is a man who loves kids, who loves education, and who knows that education is both a vitally important and a sensationally fun endeavor. From the great debate over the pros and cons of Velcro-fastened sneakers to the wisdom of John Dewey, readers of *A Child in the Principal's Office* will be engaged while laughing and learning.

JUDY WOODRUFF
ALBERT R. HUNT

Acknowledgments

I am indebted to Judy Woodruff, Anchor and Senior Correspondent at *CNN*, and Albert R. Hunt, Executive Editor of the *Wall Street Journal*, for writing the foreword to this book—a special thank you goes to them.

I also would like to offer my thanks to David Kendall, for inspiring me to write this book; David Vise, for encouraging me to finish it; Jaynie Rawl, for helping at every step; and Trustman Senger, for providing editorial assistance.

Acknowledgment is made to the following for permission to reprint previously published material by Richard Lodish:

"The Sad Results of Broken Ties," copyright © 1985 the *Washington Post*. Reprinted with permission.

"The Scarsdale Schoolroom," copyright © 1992 the *Washington Post*. Reprinted with permission.

"More Dignity for Teachers in Film, Please." A shorter version originally published in *The New York Times*, copyright © 1988 The New York Times Company. Reprinted by permission.

"Casting for Kids," copyright © 1993 Richard Lodish. Originally published in *Independent School*, Fall 1993.

In addition, the following material was originally published in *Principal* magazine:

"Debunking the Either/Or Myth," copyright © 1994 Richard Lodish, November 1994.

"Parents and Teachers: Good But Not Perfect," copyright © 1990 Richard Lodish, November 1990.

"It All Looks So Easy," copyright © 1991 Richard Lodish, May 1991.

"A Principal Buys a Dog," copyright © 1989 Richard Lodish, May 1989.

About the Author

Richard Lodish has been principal of the Sidwell Friends Lower School (Grades Pre-K through 4) since 1976 and associate headmaster of the Sidwell Friends School (Grades Pre-K through 12) since 1992. His work on educational matters, including articles in the *Washington Post* and *The New York Times,* has been published widely, and he holds a doctorate from the Harvard University Graduate School of Education. He has taught in the Cleveland Public Schools and at Catholic and Tufts Universities, formerly hosted a children's television program, and has directed institutes for beginning teachers as well as advanced leadership seminars for administrators.

He has served as consultant to the U. S. Department of Education and was an Education Policy Fellow at the Institute for Educational Leadership. After receiving a National Distinguished Principal Award from the U. S. Department of Education in 1993, he was a member of Leadership in Washington in 1994-1995 and has been a consultant in Beijing, China, where he helped to establish a bilingual, intercultural school. Sidwell Friends Lower School was recognized as an exemplary school by the U.S. Department of Education in 1986.

Lodish has served on many educational advisory boards, including the Disney Salute to the American Teacher and City at Peace, and he is also a member of many service organizations, overseeing soup kitchens, a men's shelter, and a bilingual preschool.

Introduction

Teaching children is serious business. More than ever in American schools, serious words need to be uttered, serious thoughts need to be formulated, and serious changes need to be made. But as T. S. Eliot said, "Humor is also a way of saying something serious." I think schools would be more successful if they combined serious learning with more laughter, more gaiety, more joy, more good old-fashioned humor. Where these qualities are in balance is where children learn best. As my Grandma Fanny told me, "Richie dear, remember, the books will change, the theories will change, the ideas about teaching will change, but the *kinder*, the children, will remain the same." It is for the child in all of us that I write this book.

In the midst of today's rhetorical debates on education, I think American parents and educators could use a little levity—the kind that, in the best of schools, brightens their children's lives. Thus, this book on education attempts to be both humorous and informative, poking fun at American education while addressing its themes and issues. As I examine our elementary schools, I hope to provide comic relief from the stresses of parenting and teaching.

This book offers a way for me to tell stories as well as to savor and appreciate the particulars—the voices and faces of kids and the nitty-gritty of classrooms that I have encountered in my 20 years as principal of Sidwell Friends Lower School, an independent day school in Washington, DC. It is these snapshots from my experience that this book offers. I hope these stories provide some insight for parents and other educators into what really makes schools run. It is not a how-to manual; it is one principal's reflections on schooling, his own child-hood, what he has learned, and how he has learned it.

Since I became Lower School principal at Sidwell Friends School, I have kept a log of my amusing and bizarre school experiences, as well as those that have prompted me to revisit my own childhood memories. Many of these experiences and memories were described to Sidwell Friends parents in the form of monthly letters. This book is essentially an outgrowth of these letters, a few essays per month, from September through August, although here I have added some of the saltier stories that I would never dare tell parents at my school.

It's strange how we end up in our professions. When I was in school, if there had been a category for the student least likely to become a principal, I would have been nominated—and I would have won hands down!

I remember putting a glass of water on the top of my teacher's door so that when she opened it, water would spill on her head. I remember marching the wrong way on the football field during halftime, banging my bass drum, to the uproarious laughter of a stadium full of people chanting, "Lodi, Lodi," and the teacher bellow-ing in his thick German accent, "Loddish, git owt ov my band! Loddish, git owt ov my band!" I remember doing a rain dance during our second-grade visit to the fire station to the boisterous laughter of the kids (and even the firemen), and then having to spend 2 days in first grade as punishment.

I remember listening to a Cleveland Indians play-off game while crouched in the back of an assembly with a contraband transistor radio when the principal bellowed, "Okay, who has that darn radio?" "I do, sir," I mumbled. "Okay, Lodish," he admonished, "go to my office NOW!" As I shuffled towards the door, he added loudly, "By the way, what's the score?"

After spending, on average, one period a day being a child in the principal's office, I finally made it to my senior year in high school, where I spent one period a day in a locker. During my stint as a hall guard, I reluctantly would hide in lockers while Ronnie Presser, the burly son of the head of the local Teamsters Union and the younger brother of Jackie Presser, the late and infamous head of the national Teamsters, brought intimidated students over to reenact various epi-sodes from *Candid Camera*. Some days I would scream from inside the locker, "Help me, help me! I'm from Mars. I've been in here 10 years.

Let me out, let me out!" Other days I'd squirt water through the bottom vent on little eighth graders or drop money through the top vent. Another favorite gambit of Ronnie's was to scare the daylights out of an eighth grader by telling the hapless kid that his hall pass was forged and that it had to be checked through the newly installed hall pass machine—my locker. After he dropped the hall pass in the top vent, I would make grinding and churning machine-like noises, write "NO" on the hall pass and slide it out the bottom vent. Then we would send the terrified kid to the principal's office and tell him to report that he had been caught forging a hall pass.

For years, I was made to believe (taught?) that my humorous escapades had caused me to miss out on my "real" education. But the latest research has finally vindicated me! In an article in the *Washington Post* titled "Laughing It Up: Nothing Very Subtle About Kids' Humor,"[1] "strict humor theorists" report finding evidence that a sense of humor may enhance a child's learning and creativity as well as boost the body's ability to fight pain and illness. These humor specialists further note that laughing at the incongruities in a child's world, especially the ones that make them uneasy, helps them deal with stress and frustration, as well as learn to solve problems and relate successfully to their peers. If "humor is," as reported, "one of the most reliable means we have of gauging a child's development," then, according to my mom, little Richie must have been advanced for his age!

Perhaps being a principal has given me a chance to get even—and for the kids to get even with me. Just last week, I went into a classroom and Jimmy yelled, "Don't let Mr. Lodish in here. He takes our candy from the estimating jar." There is method to my madness of purposely injecting humor whenever I can (okay, occasionally I can go to extremes). We live in a tense world, our schools should be rigorous, education is a serious business, and hard work isn't always fun—nor should it be. I agree, I agree. But, darn it, we also need to loosen up, to prance around, to act silly. I hadn't thought of humor in such an erudite manner before, but I've come to realize that we need to laugh at our kids, with our kids, and let them laugh at us. We need to enjoy the bonding that occurs when we make someone else laugh and understand that humor can bring us closer together. And isn't that all a big part of a balanced education—to balance the academic side with the fun side, heavy learning with light-headed laughter? Because too many kids today pass school and flunk life, we need to heed the advice of the humor specialists: "If we show children the lighter side of life as a child, they're more likely to grow up as fun-loving people."[2]

A series of coincidences brought me to my present position. I taught in the Cleveland public schools for 4 years (first grade, second grade, and a class for behavioral problems), and memories of those times are intertwined in this book. After spending 4 years completing my doctorate at the Harvard Graduate School of Education, I just happened to be in the placement office when the then-head of Sidwell Friends School called and, to make a long story short, I received a free trip to Washington. My daughter had just been born, my wife liked Washington, and, most important, I realized it was one of the few schools where the philosophy—Quaker philosophy, as it turns out—was completely compatible with my own.

When I arrived at Sidwell Friends School 20 years ago, I literally sat in my office for 3 days, twiddling my thumbs and asking myself, "What do I do now?" I learned quickly. The phones began to ring, and parents started complaining. On one line, Mrs. Carpenter wanted her child out of Miss A's class and into Mrs. B's. On the other line, Mrs. Churney wanted her child out of Mrs. B's class and into Miss A's class. Other parents wanted nitrates out of hot dogs; homework out of first grade; the picture book *Where Do Babies Come From?* out of the library; and roaches out of the classroom without pesticides. Of course, teachers wanted these complaining parents out of their rooms altogether. I recently reread my first letter to parents, in which I quoted Benjie Sheinkman, a fourth grader, "Mr. Lodish is the principal of our school (what else?). He is understanding and he's always working. However . . . this is only the beginning of the year; as far as I'm concerned, there's always a good 50 percent chance that I might be sent to his office and God knows what'll happen then." And this year, Anna Schwartz asked her mother (this is all true) if I got paid for what I did. Her mother told her, "Yes, of course." Anna then asked, "Does he get paid less than the teachers?" "No," responded her mother. Anna retorted, "Well, my goodness, he should be paid less. After all, he walks around and tells jokes and acts like a child in his office."

These 20 years have been an incredible personal journey. When one stays that long in a school, one's values and personality inevitably have an effect on the curriculum and tone. What I have tried to do is keep the philosophy of the school alive and my own growth compatible with that philosophy. I've been fortunate in my job in that there have been few constraints imposed from above. Yet there are times when I feel like a mushroom in the dark, covered by manure, with people stepping on me all the time and lots of people—mostly parents—wanting to chop off my head.

After 20 years in one institution, the cast of characters gets very well known, with few secrets kept. Case in point: For the first time, this year I took 4 personal days to go to the beach with my family during the school year. When I came back and opened my office door, everything—chairs, tables, couch—had been removed and replaced by 50 pounds of sand, beach balls, dead fish, lounge chairs, a cooler, a pitcher of margaritas, an inflatable raft, sea shells, a huge beach umbrella, a boom box, and a copy of the *National Enquirer* for easy beach reading.

With all these shenanigans occurring, what is Sidwell Friends like as a school? Actually, it is a serious yet joyful academic environment. The spiritual support of our Quaker philosophy helps us to balance and keep in perspective our pursuit of the paradox of lively calm and tranquil excitement. Our Quaker philosophy, which has been part of the Sidwell Friends School for 100 years and part of other Quaker institutions for 300 years, provides a framework for our efforts, but the special nature of the school, which is so stimulating to children and teachers alike, is this dynamic balance. The teaching of basic skills, for which our school is nationally recognized, is balanced by our encouragement of individual creative expression through a lively and thematically designed curriculum where art, music, reading, writing, math, and science reinforce one another, where children begin to form their own opinions based on sound and reasoned judgment, and where respect for ideas is as important as respect for authority. Most important, we strive to create an environment that emphasizes spiritual and human values and one in which the Quaker aspects of our school are not just vague, empty words. For example, every Wednesday for the past 10 years, students have worked together to make a 50-gallon pot of soup to be served at Martha's Table, a soup kitchen and children's center. Older children work with younger children peeling potatoes and cutting carrots. And on regularly scheduled Saturdays, parents, children, grandparents, and teachers meet at Martha's Table to prepare food and assist with the children's programs.

Sidwell Friends has been labeled as a "prestigious" private school ever since Archibald Roosevelt, President Teddy Roosevelt's son, matriculated in 1904, and especially since Chelsea Clinton, daughter of President Clinton, recently enrolled. Yet we have an incredible cross section of children from all religions and backgrounds—about a third of whom are now termed children "of color" and 20% of whom receive financial assistance. As *The Los Angeles Times* put it, "Although the Clintons were criticized by some public school advocates for shunning a public education in favor of a private one, Sidwell's diverse student body and its emphasis on community service made the decision more acceptable for many liberals. Having declared his intention to improve the nation's schools, the President could decide to incorporate some of what he sees at Sidwell into any school reform initiative his administration undertakes."[3]

With all of the well-known people around our school, we have to be careful that we don't suffer from secondhand fame. I remember a few years ago when I came into my office one morning to find it had been taken over by two national TV reporters and a congressman—all three parents at our school—who were discussing and filming a late-breaking story. I also remember a particularly heated social studies class where the kids were discussing an article about one child's father that was written by his classmate's mother and published in a newspaper owned by another's grandmother. Another time I had to page a congressman to ask him to take home his son, whose head lice had infected an entire classroom. We also have prominent and not-so-prominent parents whose kids spend a great deal of time in the principal's office—as I did—and who would just as soon attend back-to-school nights under assumed names.

Working in an independent school such as Sidwell Friends and having attended and taught in public schools has posed a dilemma for me, and, in fact, the book tiptoes around the private-public school issue. Perhaps I've rationalized that the Quaker aspects of this school have, in a sense, made it less elitist, but in my reflective moments, I do harbor some "guilt," which I think is healthy. Before coming to Sidwell Friends, the only other time I had stepped foot inside an independent school was for 1 hour when I was in junior high school. My friend Mike Baron had a girlfriend at Hathaway Brown, a fancy all-girl prep school in Cleveland. Mike, who had whiskers and looked old beyond his years, dressed as a plumber, complete with overalls and a tool belt. As his "apprentice," I hitchhiked with Mike to Hathaway Brown, where we walked into his girlfriend's class and, to the delight of the girls and the consternation of the teachers, we banged on the radiators, flicked switches, and twisted nozzles. After a 1-hour interrogation by the principal, we were strongly urged to leave.

We in independent schools can avoid some of the huge problems that so many public schools are experiencing, but more important, we can be a lighthouse for educational innovation. Because of our independence and capacity for flexibility, we can implement more than just an add-water-and-stir curriculum. We can define our own mission and purpose, what we are and what we are not, and what we seek to do and why, without regard to current educational fads or unreasonable parent demands.

Sidwell Friends Lower School was honored recently with an Excellence in Education award by the U.S. Department of Education. One of the reasons we applied for this award was that I want our school to help build new bridges between the public and private sectors. In spite of—indeed, because of—our differences, we have a lot to learn from and share with one another. As a wit once said, "We should be loving critics and critical lovers." Ernest Boyer, former Commissioner of Education, stated in an address to the Friends Council on Education, "Friends schools are committed ethically and socially and spiritually to serve all children. . . . And above all, they stress the point of values and using learning to engage in service. So, I think indeed the tradition of Quaker education, if I might put it so bluntly, is precisely what the public schools are groping for in order to establish both quality and purpose."[4]

Sidwell Friends continues its efforts to get away from what historically has been the smug insularity of independent schools. As a recent National Distinguished Principal honoree, I had the opportunity to spend 3 days with 50 other National Distinguished Principals selected by the Department of Education and national education associations, most of whom represented public schools—one per state—around the country. Not once did I hear educational jargon; rather, these principals—many working in extraordinarily difficult environments—stressed the simple messages of helping children to learn, helping parents to feel a part of the school community, caring about kids, and putting in place a demanding curriculum. These principals clearly loved what they were doing and felt they had touched the lives of children and their families. Many of them had been offered higher-level administrative jobs and had turned them down in order to have direct influence on and contact with kids, teachers, and parents.

In one roundtable session, I asked these great principals (they truly should be nationally distinguished) what they would do differently if they were able to have their own schools apart from the bureaucratic constraints of a large system. They all spoke of eliminating tenure, being able to choose their own faculty, doing away with grades on report cards (even if parents would be upset because Pizza Hut would stop giving students free pizzas for As), more parent-teacher conferences, flexibility to design their own curricula and manage their own budgets, fewer mandated directives from above, and the ability to give more power to their teachers. Later that night, in his address to our group, Richard Riley, the U.S. Secretary of Education, confirmed what these principals had been saying all day, that we "need to loosen the reins for principals and teachers to make things happen for the good of children." What I kept hearing is that, regardless of elaborate curriculum plans, organizational models, and accountability systems (some of which, in fact, have succeeded in our schools), the most important aspect of a school is getting outstanding people to be in the trenches and letting them do what they do best—as the 1960s song advises—"Teach your children well."

One of my favorite stories about education is that of a principal in a small rural town who had prepared a lengthy speech for an evening meeting with parents. Arriving at his school at 8:00, he saw only one parent in the audience. More than a bit discouraged, he started to pack up his speech and his various audiovisual materials and prepared to leave, when the one gentleman stood up and said, "Mr. Principal, I get up every morning at 4:30 and feed my cows. I walk a half mile to the barn to get out the feed. If only one cow shows up, I still feed that cow." The principal got the point, and for an hour and a half he talked about school philosophy, organization, curriculum, and teachers; he showed slides, overhead transparencies, and charts. When he was done, the farmer stood up and said, "Mr. Principal, I get up every morning at 4:30 to feed the cows; I walk a half mile to the barn and put out the feed. If only one cow shows up, I still feed her, but dammit, I don't give her the whole load!"

This book provides snapshots of Sidwell Friends School, but it certainly is not intended to present the whole load. The closest I come to the "whole load" is in Chapter 2, where I discuss the infamous Lodish Hit. (For those of you who may be humor-impaired, go directly to the end of Chapter 2 and repeat "whole Lodish Hit" quickly five times.)

For those of you who want to start with chapter 1, please proceed—but brace yourself for the beginning of another school year. I'm sure you remember that mixture of excitement and dread, that empty twinge in the pit of your stomach each September. You think it's bad for the kids, well, think of the guy who has to face them. Think of the child in the principal's office.

RICHARD LODISH

Flannery O'Connor once said that anybody who has survived childhood has enough material to last them the rest of their lives. Not that we would be writing about our childhoods the rest of our lives, but that childhood is a time of deep impressions, and there is a tendency to replicate those early experiences in our adult lives.

DENNIS MCFARLAND[5]

September

1

Richard's Inability to Mature

During my years of growing up and teaching in Cleveland, Ohio, my entire being underwent a strange metamorphosis early each September. Innocuous but continual blasts from the airwaves by the now-bankrupt Robert Hall Company signaled the change: "School bells ringing . . . children singing . . . it's back to Robert Hall again. . . . Mother knows for better clothes . . . it's back to Robert Hall again."

Now, two days before the children arrive at school, for reasons that $150 sessions on a Freudian couch couldn't pry out of my psyche, the jingle reappears to haunt me. The beginning of another school year has arrived.

And the morning before school begins, I am reminded of this tender exchange between a mother and her son:

> "Ma, I don't want to go to school today. The kids don't like me, the parents hate me, the teachers despise me. I don't want to go to school."

> "Son," replied his mother, "you have to go to school today—you're the principal."

Yes, for 20 years I've had to go to school. I'm the principal.

I've been in more than a few principals' offices in my time—currently on my own accord as The Principal. A while back—well, let's just say it was not always on my own accord. My office wall tells the rest. Most principals' office walls have a diploma or two, an occa-sional lithograph, maybe a student's painting. Venture into my office. Several years ago I houselifted from my parents' bottom dresser drawer my third-grade report card. Upon discovering my pilfering, my mom exclaimed, "Richie, don't you dare show that to anyone. You're the principal now!" Contrary to Mom's wishes and encased neatly in plexiglass, Miss Hazelett's 1954 report card for Richard Lodish, Taylor School, hangs in Mr. Lodish's office:

> How disappointed we are in Richard's inability to mature. He not only spoils his own work, but makes it hard for his friends to do their best. If Richard would try to help others, even one day, I believe he would enjoy it enough to make it a habit. Of course, living the Cub Scout way is part of it.

After talking with (or perhaps mildly threatening) my parents, Miss Hazelett wrote under second semester: "He has been making an effort. He must know how happy he makes us when he is thoughtful of others. We are expecting Richard to live up to earnest plans." Earnest plans? I'm the principal now.

In 1955, upon graduating from Miss Hazelett's room (in the footsteps of my two older brothers, whose rearing was producing more positive results), I overheard my mom telling my dad, "Nate, Nate . . . Harvey never did it, Lenny never did such things. Nate, Nate, the little one—he's a wild thing, a wild thing." Yes, this wild thing is now king of 300 wild things—I'm the principal now.

* * *

Next to my third-grade report card, two pink, green, orange, and blue blobs drawn in semiabstract style with iridescent chalk on black construction paper hang on my office wall. Cecily, the 5-year-old artist, dictated the following caption to her kindergarten teacher and pasted it underneath the picture: "This is the King and he is sitting in his chair. One day he went to school and he said, 'I don't want to be the King anymore, I want to be the principal.' "

In accepting the Caldecott Medal for *Where the Wild Things Are*, Maurice Sendak, the famous author-illustrator, said, "It is my involvement with . . . the awful vulnerability of children and their struggle to make themselves king of all 'wild things' that gives my work whatever truth and passion it may have."[1]

These two quotations speak to a dilemma I face every day as principal, as I do my job without a throne or crown or worshippers at my feet. So much of my job—if I let it—can slip into simply managing my part of the Elementary School Kingdom. For a person looking after 300 young kings of all wild things, the pursuit of passion and truth can be forgotten in the tidal wave of helter-skelter minutiae. Obviously, a school has to run smoothly, things have to be done right, but a school also has to know where it is going and why the journey has been undertaken—it has to be doing the right things.

My most important function as principal is to see that we continue to pursue this goal of doing right by children, elusive as it is, with as much passion and truth as we can muster. These young wild and kingly voyagers need us to aspire to great things as well. They need to be shown by example and deeds what to value as much as they need to be shown how to blend consonants and add fractions. And that is the part of my job that gives my work whatever truth and passion it may have and makes it, well, sort of kingly.

Yessirree, this wild thing is now the king of all wild things—a child enthroned in the principal's office.

2

A Lodish Hit

During the first few weeks of school, I open car doors in carpool line to greet our newly arriving little ones and their parents. Well, a few weeks ago, I opened a car door and a Pre-K'er scooted out and vanished. His mother, unaware of her 4-year-old's rapid departure, mistakenly (I think) looked at me and said, "Have a nice day, sweetie. I love you." She then pursed her lips and made kissy-kissy sounds. Fortunately, I had learned in principal school not to pursue the matter further.

After reading how they hire principals nowadays, I should be glad that my superiors took me aboard 20 years ago and let me weather the gusty winds through so many beginning years. For I have recently read a slew of articles on an "innovative" process for hiring principals. Centers are now used to screen out the not-so-worthy from the ranks of aspiring principals. The methods they use, according to the *Washington Post*, were first developed by the German army and used later by the American intelligence community as a screening process to hire spies.

> The best way to identify a promising spy was to put him or her into simulated situations which tested tolerance for stress and the ability to solve problems under pressure—qualities needed behind enemy lines. Later, U.S. industry adopted the simulation process to hire executives. And now the National Association of . . . School Principals has applied it to school administrator recruitment.[2]

Richard Lodish assessed for qualities needed behind enemy lines? On second thought, tolerance for stress, solving problems under pressure, operating behind enemy lines—the assessment process might have helped me. But over the years, and especially during the first week of school, I have learned at least a few tricks of the trade to get me out of jams.

1. *Set rules quickly.* One fall, our fourth-grade teacher discovered graffiti on a wall in the boys' bathroom announcing, "I have a 12-inch dick." Outraged, I brought all the fourth-grade boys together and told them if the perpetrator confessed immediately, he would just have to wash off the words, but if the child didn't confess, I'd call his parents when I determined who the culprit was. No one confessed.

As part of my investigation, I gave a pencil and paper to each boy and told them all to write, "I have a 12-inch ruler" on the paper so I could match the handwriting. Before pencil struck paper, John Patrick started crying, "I'll never do it again. I'll never do it again." True to my word, I called his mother, a well-known lobbyist on Capitol Hill.

I put through the call and asked for Mrs. Raul (not her real name). The secretary replied that she was in an important meeting. I identified myself and told her that I needed to speak to Mrs. Raul immediately. Answering the phone breathlessly, Mrs. Raul asked me what was wrong. "John Patrick is okay," I responded, "but he did write some graffiti in the boys' bathroom." "What did he write?" she asked. Hesitantly, I whispered, "I have a 12-inch dick." I asked her to speak to John Patrick that evening and told her I would call her the next day.

The next day, I telephoned Mrs. Raul and was told again by the secretary that she was at an important meeting. I explained once more who I was. When Mrs. Raul came to the phone, I asked her what she had said to John Patrick. "I told him to behave in school, listen to his teachers," she replied, "and, oh yes, I told him that he can't wear Bermuda shorts."

2. *Read folders carefully.* Each fall, in the first weeks of school, I review folders of the previous year's new students. To keep me honest as I cull through 600 or so pages of progress reports sent to parents, a teacher occasionally puts in a ringer. This one crossed my desk:

Name: Willard Sutton, Jr.   Grade: 2

It is obvious that the apple does not fall far from the tree. Willie is streetwise and excitable. His participation in class is of an undetermined nature. He values his many friends; you can bank on Willie to hoodwink and bamboozle them at every opportunity. . . . Willie brings balance to our class. He is the missing link we've all been searching for. . . . Willie approaches all new subjects with an open mouth. . . . He has a good ear for reading and a good eye for music. . . . He approaches open-minded problem solving with a closed mind.

3. *Don't accept "overdue" requests.* Our school policy is that a child must be five by October 1 to enter kindergarten. After telling Mrs. Klinger that her son Sam, who would not be five until November 2, was too young for kindergarten, I received this note:

Dear Mr. Lodish:

This is to inform you that, although Sam was born on November 2, he was overdue. My due date was actually September 28. Because he would have been five by October 1, I hope you will consider Sam for kindergarten. Thank you.

Ellen Klinger

4. *Don't overrate your name or use it in vain.* When I taught in the Cleveland inner-city public schools, I was the outsider—especially to my students. I made learning "relevant" by using lyrics of current R&B songs like "My Girl" and "Dock of the Bay" to teach reading. The students and I would pick out the hit records together from the top 10 soul songs, and I would project the lyrics on the overhead projector as my students would sing along and read the lyrics. All seemed to be going fine until third grader Russell Reese remarked, "Mr. Lodish, if I made a hit record, they'd call it a 'Reese Hit.' If Richard Sullivan made a hit record, they'd call it a 'Sullivan Hit.' If Victor Jordan made a hit record, they'd call it a 'Jordan Hit.' Mr. Lodish, what would they call it if you made a hit record?" Unwittingly, I took my name in vain as I blurted out to my hysterical students, "A Lodish hit." So much for classroom control.

3

Debunking the Either/Or Myth

This fall, I was inducted into my high school Hall of Fame. In introducing the awardees, the principal admonished the students, "I want you to listen, learn, and emulate them." As I began my speech to 400 students, I expressed some concern with the principal's use of the conjunction *and*. "You should listen to me, perhaps learn a few things from what I will say, but you probably don't want to emulate me." With the principal ready to gaff me off the stage, I spoke of my rather checkered high school career. That is, the time that I was actually in high school and not at Wally's Pool Hall or Randall Race Track.

Last summer, I returned to Cleveland to attend my 30th high school reunion, where the same principal embarrassed me in front of my former classmates by telling them I was the only one from their class in the Hall of Fame. My wittier classmates immediately dubbed it the Hall of *Shame* award and shouted, "Lodi [my high school nickname], how could you have been so crazy then *and* be a principal now?" The conjunction *and* bothered them as well.

What really made the occasion extraordinary was that the only teacher who came to see his former students was Mr. Buffalini, who taught me in elementary school. He's one of only a few teachers I remember who deeply respected and cared about us and—in funny and bizarre ways—engaged us in learning. When I told him some 40 years later what a profound influence he had on my own teaching, he responded, "You guys made my teaching such a thrill that I had to come back. Lodish, you were crazy back then and yet I always thought you might become an educator." He too knew the value of the conjunction *and*; it signals that you can simultaneously possess what at first glance appear to be conflicting qualities.

Schools are full of strange juxtapositions. Kids do not separate life into *either/or*s; at their tender ages, they instead delight in the *and*s that life offers. Recently, I asked our fourth graders to jot down what thoughts came to their minds when asked what they wanted to be. Their responses included many *and*s, very few *but*s. "I want to be a peacemaker *and* develop a cure for cancer"; "I want to own a tackle shop *and* be an astrophysicist"; "I want to drive a race car *and* be a doctor"; "I'd like to be a person you can trust *and* help people, maybe like a lawyer." And finally, "I want to live all around the world when I grow up *and* not worry about taxes." (Perhaps he should hire the lawyer!)

Barry Raebeck, in the article "The School as a Humane Business,"[3] argues that schools need to change from *either/or* institutions to *and* environments. According to Raebeck, schools are too often either serious and sterile or casual and somewhat pleasant; either businesslike and efficient or humane and inefficient. Subjects are either rigorous, painful, and therefore worthwhile, or they are enjoyable, casual, and therefore frivolous.

In a new book, *The Leadership Paradox: Balancing Logic and Artistry in Schools*,[4] Terrence Deal and Kent Peterson argue that principals also need to reconcile conflicting *but*s or *either*s and make them into *and*s. They advocate educational leaders who have both technical expertise *and* the expressive touch of an artist; who can encourage dispersed *and* centered leadership; who can create cohesive communities *and* be sensitive to increasingly heterogeneous populations; who can combine strong managerial skills *and* sensitivity and passion; and who can be both jurist *and* healer.

I hope in the years to come that we debunk the myth of *either/or*. The best schools are places with both quality *and* humanity, high productivity *and* high sensitivity. We need to make certain that our children work hard *and* enjoy their work; that we assist kids who do not meet our standards *and* insist that standards not be lowered; that we expect our students to be taught basic skills *and* allow for individual creative expression; that we value individuality *and* community, self-expression *and* self-discipline, diversity *and* commonality, humor *and* seriousness, work *and* play.

We need to balance and keep in perspective the paradox of lively calm and tranquil excitement. We need our schools to be alive with spirit and yet spiritual; noisy with learning and quiet with reflection; full of independent thinkers and thinkers who are receptive to the ideas of others; brimming with joyful learners and serious pursuers of knowledge.

Having survived such contradictions in my own life, I know that it is possible to transform the limiting *either/ors* in our schools to creative *ands*. In doing so, we can help make children's learning years wonderfully productive *and* fun filled.

October

4

Parents and Teachers: Good but Not Perfect

The best advice I ever received for dealing with parents during October conference days came from across the table: You believe half of what our kids tell you about us and we'll believe half of what our kids tell us about you. I've also learned it's best to (a) not let parents congregate in groups of more than two, and (b) keep the five parents who dislike you away from the 50 new parents who are still ambivalent about you.

A few years back, *People Weekly* wrote about Prince William, son of Prince Charles and heir to the heir to the British throne, "Will's academic performance . . . is not quite on a par with his horsemanship. But his presence in Weatherby's less advanced group, the class known as Form Three Red, causes no distress to his parents." His father reportedly said, "Being too bright can be a positive disadvantage for the sort of life that William has before him . . . We're open-minded about William and his education."[1] I would have traded a dozen graduate courses in conferencing techniques to sit in at the next Weatherby parent-teacher conference to observe how the Form Three Red teacher dealt with the open and distress-free minds of Prince Charles, Princess Diana, and, I imagine, Prince William's nanny.

It's not easy being a parent these days, even for the royal family. And it's certainly not easy being a teacher these days, be it at Weatherby or at PS 101.

In most parent-teacher contacts, subtle disagreements over what constitutes good parenting and good teaching are inevitable. But what intrigues me are the roles that parents and teachers adopt as they see each other's imperfections.

In a lecture at the University of Illinois, Lillian Katz explained some of those differences:

- Teachers have a limited responsibility for children—essentially to make sure they learn and that they're secure and comfortable. Parents, on the other hand, have an unlimited responsibility; almost everything matters to them. They're with their children year after year; they can't simply resign or retire.
- Teachers should be somewhat detached from their students. If they don't keep some distance, they get too involved and burn out. But parents should be attached to their children. They can have intense feelings about them, ranging from warmth to rage, from silliness to anger.
- Teachers should be rational and intentional when they teach children. Parents are allowed to be irrational and spontaneous.
- Teachers should be impartial. They have to respect the specialness of each child, but they cannot single out one for special treatment—a "teacher's pet." Parents, on the other hand, should be biased; they should be the leaders of their child's fan club.

Recently, I asked some fourth graders to describe what they thought were the differences between parents and teachers. Here's what they said:

"Parents tell old jokes and you're supposed to laugh. Teachers tell new funny jokes and make you laugh."

"Teachers are mainly interested in things you don't know; parents are proud of you and show off things you do know."

"Teachers admit when they are wrong; parents just bluff their way through."

"Sometimes parents love you so much they get angry at you and scream at you; teachers don't get quite that angry."

"Parents sometimes seem to worry about you all the time (even nag you); teachers care about you, but don't overprotect you."

"Parents seem to always have something to hide; teachers tell you all you need to know."

"Teachers get mad at you for not doing your homework; parents get mad because they're in a bad mood."

"Parents tell you you did well on something when you really didn't; teachers only say so when you really did."

"Teachers will tell you one thing and won't tell you another; parents tell you one thing and then change their minds."

"Teachers keep you quiet and well behaved for six hours a day, something a parent could never do."

"Parents and teachers both lecture you. Parents do it longer; teachers do it really fast."

I sincerely hope that all went well during the royal parent-teacher conferences at Weatherby.

And I certainly hope that Roald Dahl's fictional depiction of parent-teacher interactions in the introduction to his book *Matilda* never comes true:

It's a funny thing about mothers and fathers. Even when their child is the most disgusting little blister you could ever imagine, they still think that he or she is wonderful.

Some parents go further. They become so blinded by adoration they manage to convince themselves their child has qualities of genius.

School teachers suffer a good deal from having to listen to this sort of twaddle. . . . If I were a teacher I would cook up some real scorchers for the children of doting parents. . . . "It is a curious truth that grasshoppers have their hearing organs in the sides of the abdomen. Your daughter, Vanessa, judging by what she's learnt this term, has no hearing organs at all."

I think I might enjoy writing end-of-term reports for the stinkers in my class. But enough of that. We have to get on.[2]

We have to get on with our roles of being good (not perfect) parents and good (not perfect) teachers.

5

The Sad Results of Broken Ties

Being a "good enough" parent sometimes is still not good enough. Witness this custody order that crossed my desk:

> *Further ordered, that the parties shall take no action against the best interests of the child and shall not seek to alienate the child's affections from either parent, and the parties shall make all efforts to resolve their differences so as to keep in mind the best interests of the child at all times.*

Life is no longer a game of kick-the-can; mommies and daddies are playing hardball now. By the time my students graduate from high school, at least 40% of their parents, the experts say, will end up separating. Divorce has made it into the big leagues, and as an elementary school principal, I have become a family umpire by default.

Nowadays, I'm called upon to decide who sits with whom at school performances. Recently, Mrs. Reed pleaded with me to find out where her former husband was sitting at a school play. After my reconnaissance, I cautiously escorted her to the other side of the auditorium, praying that the only "scene" would be the one her daughter was in on the stage.

I even referee family feuds. Waking me up at 6:00 a.m. with the news that her husband had just shoved a 20-foot ladder up to their kid's bedroom, a hysterical parent pleaded with me not to let her husband visit the school that morning. Five minutes later, the husband called me, complaining that when he rang the doorbell to his house, his wife shoved him down the front stairs. Now what the heck is this umpire by default supposed to do? Perhaps I should charge hundreds of dollars per hour like the lawyers and shrinks, or maybe I should just repeat to parents the old saw that in marriage, like banking, there's a penalty for early withdrawal.

I began thinking about divorce and its effects on children while I was in graduate school 25 years ago. My wife and I were sitting on the stoop of our Cambridge apartment when we overheard a passing father say matter-of-factly to his small son, "Daddy loves you. Mommy loves you. It's just that Mommy doesn't love Daddy anymore."

Maybe my sensitivity to divorce has been heightened by my job, but since that event, I see divorce all around us. The lawyers, the psychologists, the demographers, the educators, and the counselors submit their theories about the causes of the increasing divorce rate. Statistics are compiled, conferences are held, and documents are written. I've read the documents; I've been on panels; I've attended workshops.

Yet in looking through the great bulk of expert opinion and the masses of statistics on the increasing rate of divorce, there is a failure to recognize that divorce has unobtrusively drifted into the category of thoroughly familiar and somehow acceptable phenomena. It's difficult to attend a movie, turn on the TV, or read a newspaper or magazine without divorce creeping in. There is not a neat beginning, middle, or end to this divorce creepage in our media-drenched society. But certain events, such as the porch episode in Cambridge, have stayed with me, perhaps as harbingers of the future.

July 1, 1975. Ann Landers, adviser of advisers, the champion of family life, announced just short of her 36th wedding anniversary that she and her husband were divorcing.

May 24, 1980. Anita Bryant, the symbol of Florida orange juice, whose ministry was to preserve the American family, took action against her mate.

I remember watching Sonny and Cher performing together on a variety show ogling one another and ogling their daughter, Chastity, on stage—after they already had proclaimed to the world that they were splitting up.

I watched the news one evening as Marie Osmond, of the close-knit Osmond family, announced on TV the unraveling of her marriage.

Now the media is drenching us with the much-touted separation of Prince Charles and Princess Diana.

And, although there has been little discussion about it, Ronald Reagan was the first divorced president in the history of the United States.

Kramer vs. Kramer was followed by a slew of movies with divorce as the central theme. Almost all movies now, although not concentrating on divorce, have at least one couple uncoupling; split-ups are as common as the old western shoot-outs.

Soap operas and the *Dallas*es aren't the only television programs that unbind celluloid families. One episode of *Family Ties* untied Uncle Bob's family knot. The TV series *Civil Wars* was all about, well, "civil" wars.

It seems there is no end to the confusion or the confessions. Recently, I listened in amazement as a mother explained that her 5-year-old was not her ex-husband's child, but that she had been artificially inseminated by an anonymous donor. That night, I had a nightmare that her mischievous child trotted into my office, flung down a test tube on my desk, and yelled, "Tell my dad what you told me, buster!"

Each of us could compile his or her own list of personal experiences that have seemed to place divorce so firmly in the center of American life. We can argue about which events are significant for whom. And, of course, there is no list of top 10 causes for divorce, no neat sequence of events that have produced our huge divorce rate.

The fact remains that divorce permeates our society, and I witness its sad effects on children every day. Regardless of joint custody, sole custody, amicable settlements, and appropriate counseling, I still see the hurt, the tension, the tears, and the behavioral problems. I understand that divorce can be the best—or the only—alternative. I understand the incompatibility of certain couples. I understand that to many adults, divorce can be seen as a kind of right, a freedom—as American as apple pie and, yes, motherhood. I understand. I understand. I understand.

The commonness of divorce has taken away some of the stigma that children used to feel, but it does nothing to relieve the pain of losing the presence of both parents in the home. If 40% of their friends also have experienced this loss, children may not feel different from their peers, but that doesn't mean they feel good. Divorce remains shocking to me no matter how much its public shock value has worn off.

For the father telling his child, "It's just that Mommy doesn't love Daddy anymore," and for the child whose fate lies in the judge's order on my desk, a hurt exists that defies explanation and rationalization. For this child and for many others who come into my principal's office, childhood is no longer a game of kick-the-can.

6

It All Looks So Easy

Parenting, divorced or otherwise, has its own set of difficulties, but teaching—real teaching—is a strange world of its own. As someone once quipped, "Teachers are nonconsenting adults involved in unnatural acts."

It all looks so easy. Twenty-five wide-eyed children, gobs of materials, piles of books, plenty of space—all the right stuff. But take my word for it, teaching—that is, real teaching—is not easy.

I have been a teacher myself, and as principal, I try to spend a lot of time in classrooms every year, sometimes as much as a full week in one class. It gives me an opportunity to observe teaching and learning, to work with children, to take notes, and to provide feedback to teachers. It all looks so easy—until you get your feet wet and your toes stubbed.

During the month of October, I substitute in many of our classes while teachers conduct parent conferences. I will not bore you with all my classroom exploits because I do not seek permanent embarrassment. After all, I am the principal. Perhaps a few examples will suffice.

In the second-grade class, I was asked to teach how lightning works as part of a unit on weather. I was given four children's books on this subject in order to review what I never really understood in the first place. After an agonizing night of homework, not only did I still not comprehend how lightning works, but I could not even provide a plausible explanation to a class of 6- and 7-year-olds.

Futilely hoping to avoid humiliation, I had the students design lightning bolts from pipe cleaners and place them on paper painted to show a stormy scene. I then went around the room stapling the lightning bolts to the papers. But when I returned to collect the finished products, the children began to laugh uncontrollably. I had stapled the lightning bolts to their desks.

In the first-grade classroom, I was asked to explain why spiders spin their webs in patterns. In the fourth grade, I was brought into a discussion of the strange mating habits of the scarab beetle, worshipped in ancient Egypt.

In my visit to Ms. McMullen's fourth-grade class, children were acting out drama cards. I finally guessed that Hannelore was opening an umbrella in a heavy wind. Never one to resist center stage, I took my turn, depicting a scene in which a naughty child comes into my office and I call his parents. Amy guessed I was acting out an old man falling down in the street. So much for center stage.

In kindergarten, I was called upon to demonstrate how to make a clay pot. I alternated rolling clay and pinching it with my fingers. Although it was a little lopsided after being fired in the kiln, I was proud of my creation. Five-year-old Jimmy smiled and said it looked good . . . NOT! When I took it home, my wife and daughter both asked me which kindergartner had given me a clay pot.

Another time, in third grade, after several bathroom calamities, Mrs. Herndon asked me to talk "guy talk" with her boys about the "correct" way to pee. I quickly hired two consultants to help! (Our phys-ed teacher and the custodian.) After trying to explain the relative merits of the "ready, fire" method versus the "ready, aim, fire" method, we temporarily lost control of the group with a fit of giggles. Nevertheless, the bathroom magically improved.

Each of these lessons confirms the experience of a famous physicist once asked to explain coupled pendulums. After talking for a while about conservation and transfer of energy, he grinned and said, "Well, I know all the right words, but I don't understand it either."

We all learn. As I visit classrooms, I am continually struck by all the learning—by both students and teachers—that occurs. In my position, I am one of the few lucky ones. Like the grandfather who plays with his grandchildren, but leaves the nitty-gritty to their parents, I have the luxury of observing the depth of preparation, the persistence, the extraordinary patience, the careful listening, the calmness, the gentleness, the deep thought, the creativity—yes, the giggles—and most of all, the passion that teachers bring to their teaching. I think it was Lillian Hellman who said, "Marriage begins with passion and ends with laundry." My experience has shown that our teachers begin with passion, and somehow that passion continues to radiate within and beyond their classrooms.

Even after 20 years as a principal, I continue to marvel not only at their expertise, but at their love of and passion for teaching. They make it all look so easy.

November

7

A Principal Buys a Dog

Okay, I bought a dog. My daughter is finally old enough and it's November, the beginning of the holiday craziness. Lots of people buy dogs, I know. But in my mind, the degree of similarity between buying and raising a dog, parenting, and teaching surpasses mere coincidence. Even my daughter, who affirms the ancient credo that no child ever keeps a promise to take care of a dog, agrees with these child-rearing/dog-rearing parallels.

The year was 1952; the place was Cleveland, Ohio. Getting a family dog was simple: a 20-minute ride to the dog pound, a sawbuck, and two shots later, Rusty was home. (Rusty was so ugly that the fleas in the neighborhood held a lottery: The winner did not have to move in with him.)

Fast-forward to November 1994; the place is Washington, DC. After 26 calls to dog clubs and breeders, two pounds of dog manuals, and an 82-mile drive to the kennel, we purchased a pedigreed Golden Retriever yuppy puppy whose genealogy includes such distinguished ancestors as Sir Charles of Twin Oaks, Fidelia Buffy, and even Honors Foxfire Liberty Hume, President Ford's mutt. We call her Khaki.

Khaki was bred to be a perfect dog. I wonder, if it weren't for genetic engineering roadblocks, whether parents would similarly opt for perfect children. But even if we could obtain kids with guarantees and pedigrees, would we really want them to be predetermined to achieve perfection? What, after all, would become of their handlers and trainers?

Teaching a puppy the basics is an important task often considered best left to entrepreneurs who cater to the "hectic work schedules of busy metropolitan residents." There were any number of puppy preschools and dog academies eager to educate my dog, including one that offered "daily in-school training, private behavior consultations, and school bus pick-up and delivery."

I found all of this unbelievable until a school parent showed me her dog's daily report card. Angel had received a poor mark that day for distractions, but with the exculpatory notation that Angel was "in heat." In heat or not, she did beat our preschoolers with a 3-minute sit-stay and a 20-second auto sit.

Are comparisons between puppy care and child care absurd? Think about it. Today, the rough, yet fulfilling job of raising kids is more often done by nannies and day care centers than by parents. One result is that today's kids are being pressured to learn more and more at younger and younger ages. It's no wonder that preschool stress syndromes are becoming as common as adult neuroses.

It seems that the folks who brought us super babies and fast-track kids are now applying their technological wizardry to producing superpups and fast-track dogs. For example, there is the electronic dog trainer, billed as completely humane and efficient, that emits enough of an electric shock to "let your dog know that you remain in control." (Just think, these could be hooked up to kids in the school lunchroom.)

No home would be complete without the no-bark trainer, a device that triggers a self-punishing jolt every time the dog barks. Yup, these gadgets could be just the thing for noisy assemblies.

Although technology can ease the task of dog rearing, it cannot replace the bond created between a dog and its owner. The same is true in teaching children. Computers and VCRs may be quite good, but they cannot take the place of a skilled and caring teacher.

When it comes to books on dog care, I think the dog experts definitely have surpassed the child care gurus in sheer chutzpah. Simply substitute "child" for "dog" in many of these books, and you have the texts for Child Care 101.

For example, I purchased a book on behavioral problems in dogs that has chapters on destructive behavior, introverted behavior, and nutritional problems. The purpose of this tome is to "help you better understand your dog." I was so impressed that I purchased copies for our resource room and school nurse.

Another book, with the intriguing title *How to Be Your Dog's Best Friend*, points out that "understanding is the key to communication with your dogs." I have made copies available to school parents.

But wait, that's not all. For our standardized testers, I plan to purchase copies of a training book in which "the dog's own cognitive abilities are cultivated and encouraged, teaching him to exercise options in order to achieve the desired behavior."

I found all of these books and gadgets (not to mention dog châteaux and haute cuisine) rather harmless until I discovered that my total expenses for Khaki were more than double the cost of a college education for the same period of time. I also discovered that I had become part of the 94% of people who talk to their dogs as if they were human and could understand us.

Parents, teachers, principals (and dogs, for all I know) are often mystified by all of the experts telling them what to do and how to do it. In the end, all of us, in our own way, with our own beliefs, strengths, and weaknesses, have to figure out what we want for our children (and for our dogs) and how to provide it.

Having said this, I would like to share my favorite and most telling chapter heading, one that has obvious implications for those parents, teachers, and principals who fumble along when it comes to raising kids. From the book *Good Dog, Bad Dog,* the chapter is titled "The Corrective Jerk."

8

That Big or Too Tough

"You are too young to help anybody and I am too old," he said. "By help I don't mean a courtesy like serving choke-cherry jelly or giving money.

"Help," he said, "is giving part of yourself to somebody who comes to accept it willingly and needs it badly.

"So it is," he said, using an old homiletic transition, "that we can seldom help anybody. Either we don't know what part to give or maybe we don't like to give any part of ourselves. Then, more often than not, the part that is needed is not wanted. And even more often, we do not have the part that is needed. It is like the auto-supply shop over town where they always say, 'Sorry, we are just out of that part.' "

I told him, "You make it too tough. Help doesn't have to be anything that big."[1]

I agree with Norman Maclean's response to his dad in his sensitive memoir of family and fishing, *A River Runs Through It*: Help doesn't have to be that big or too tough. In schools, we must teach our students helpfulness and responsibility, but we also must make certain that these lessons are not that big or too tough for our youngsters—and not taught solely during the Thanksgiving season.

I asked a third grader, "What do you want for the world? What do you want for yourself?" "For the world," he said, "I want enough food and shelter for everyone. For me, I want a GI Joe with a matching Mattel grenade launcher and a swimming pool." So works the mind of an 8-year-old. Young children are apt to entertain contradictions easily, turning ideas on their heads without being aware of any inconsistencies. The late Rene Dubois, who admonished us to "Think globally, act locally," would have been interested in this youngster's response.

We must not place the burden of the world's problems on the shoulders of 6- and 7-year-olds. Yet schools must continue to ask at what age and in what ways young children are ready to learn the painful truths about the gap between the haves and the have-nots, between our ideals and realities.

Developmental psychologists—the most prominent of them, I believe, is Lawrence Kohlberg—have studied children's moral capacity to help others. Dr. Kohlberg envisions three primary levels of moral development in childhood and beyond. At the lowest and youngest age level, we are guided by an orientation toward punishment and obedience; at the intermediate level, by the approval of others and a desire for good relations with them; and, at the highest level, by conscience. In my own life, three incidents jump out that support these three Kohlbergian levels.

Level 1. My third-grade teacher, Mrs. Hazelett, in a rare attempt at teaching goodness, instructed us to tell our mothers how much we appreciated their cooking and to volunteer to clean up afterwards. Well, I still remember muttering after that evening meal in 1954, "Ma, you sure did a great job cooking. This is a delicious dinner, and I want to clean up." My older brothers started kicking me under the table as if to say, "Don't think we're going to help, Mama's boy." My mother placed her palm on my forehead and asked if I felt sick. But I obediently followed Mrs. Hazelett's prodding and, at least for one day, I felt pretty good about lending a rare helpful hand in the Lodish household.

Level 2. I was 16 and a new driver. Jeff and I had parked in front of Drexsler's Drugs in Cleveland during a rainstorm and were about to drive away. Suddenly, the door opened and an older lady shoved two bags of groceries in the back seat, demanding, "Boychicks, take me home." Thinking for sure we were on *Candid Camera*, Jeff and I graciously helped the lady into the car and made faces in the rearview mirror. As I started to drive, she put the damper on the *Candid Camera* idea, informing us that her name was Mrs. Merowitz and that her granddaughter attended our high school. Even though Dr. Kohlberg would say I was guided by wanting the approval of others—in this case, my friend Jeff and the *Candid Camera* crew—I did a good deed and drove Mrs. Merowitz home. I even carried in her bags for her.

Level 3. Last year, early in the holiday season, I found a wallet with $520 in cash, a Coast Guard and Munitions card, and a dental appointment card from Atlanta, all with the name Terry Johnson on them. After an unsuccessful bureaucratic runaround with the Coast Guard, I called the dental office in Atlanta, where the secretary called Terry's grandmother, who in turn called Terry in Washington, giving him my name and my office and home numbers.

That afternoon, Terry called me at school. I explained that the holiday shows were going full tilt and that the best time for him to come collect his wallet was around 2:00 the next day. Fine and dandy. Well—this is all true—at 3:00 a.m. (that's *a.m.*, folks), my phone rang at home. Startled, I woke up to hear Terry saying, "Hey, man, where are you? I've been waiting at the front gate of your school for over an hour. I'm at the Giant supermarket at the pay phone now." After wiping the sleep and the astonishment out of my eyes, I met Terry at the Giant and gave him the wallet. "Hey, thanks," he said, "let me give you something." I said, "No, it's the holiday season. You be nice to somebody else and let's all try to make the world a better place." The next morning, I found a $50 bill in the back seat. Conscience got the best of both of us.

Although not as bizarre, similar moral vignettes are played out daily in our schools. Teachers must be sensitive to, but not bound by, their students' levels of moral reasoning, whether the impetus comes from a desire to be obedient (or, heaven forbid, to avoid punishment) or to gain approval, or from a developed conscience. Ultimately, we need to believe that each person has an innate capacity for goodness and a responsibility to attain that goodness. Indeed, this belief is the organizing principle around which schools should function.

By the time children are of kindergarten age, cites Alfie Kohn in his book *The Brighter Side of Human Nature: Altruism and Empathy in Everyday Life*,[2] comforting, sharing, and helping are regular occurrences. When asked why they help one another, young children most frequently offered the simple explanation that the other child "needed help." According to Alfie Kohn, this is the heart of altruism. He says, "It is enough to suggest that parents and educators hoping to raise a child who is responsive to the needs of others already have 'an ally within the child.' "[3]

We anticipate and hope that, with time, guidance, and faith, our children—our allies—will do the right thing for all the Hazeletts, Merowitzes, and Johnsons, even when helping others seems that big or too tough.

9

Be a Mensch

I wore my good suit during a Thanksgiving assembly. A third grader came up to me and said, "Mr. Lodish, you look like a principal, but I know you're nice." Regardless of Cosi's definition of "nice" or her judgment about my niceness, her comment did prompt this thought: Are educators and parents "nice," and how do we get others who are younger to be nice? Or, to use the parlance of the day, how do we offer a morally sound education?

Calvin Trillin, in a poignant article in a recent issue of *The New Yorker*, searched for the ultimate advice on becoming nice and here's what he found:

> What strikes me as odd now is how much my father managed to get across to me without those heart-to-hearts which I've read about fathers and sons having in the study or in the rowboat. . . . Somehow I understood completely how he expected me to behave in small matters as well as large, even though I can't remember being given any lectures about it beyond that occasional, undramatic "You might as well be a mensch."[4]

For those of you who don't speak Yiddish—or didn't grow up with my Bubby Fanny—Webster's defines a mensch as "One having admirable characteristics, as integrity and compassion."

To have a moral school, a school where we might as well all be "mensches," the pieces have to fit together; they have to be part of a

41

whole. Such a school must be authentic, full of daily interactions of being nice. Far too often in today's world, the pieces are out of sync.

I'm from the Woodstock generation. I thought it was an event where people treated each other nicely—perhaps a hopeful harbinger of things to come. However, I recently read in the *Washington Post* that Richie Havens, a star of Woodstock, hailed the event as "an evolutionary breakthrough—the basis for everything that's been happening on the planet ever since." On the other hand, he's suing the copyright owners of the Woodstock albums and videos for $50 million.[5]

Nationally, the moral pieces don't quite mesh, either. Former education secretary William Bennett's moralizing *Book of Virtues* has been lodged near the top of the best-seller list whereas moral decline is at the top of the political agenda. Meanwhile, House members have formed a "House Character Counts" (an oxymoron?) group to promote a resolution which aims to encourage character education in schools.

Of course, inculcating values in schools is not new. In my office are children's penmanship lessons from the 1930s, carefully copied from precepts provided by the National Institute for Moral Education. My favorite deals with "clean play": "I will not cheat nor will I play for keeps. I will treat my opponent with courtesy. If I play in a group game, I will play not for my own glory, but for the success of my team and the fun of the game. I will be a good loser or a generous winner."

While schools are searching for specific curricula and methods to teach values and morals, those pieces often stand apart from the day-to-day school climate. Recently, I was invited to a conference titled "Moral Education—An Idea Whose Time Has Come." What time is it anyway? I don't mean to sound preachy, but darn it, schools need to get their act together, to align the moral puzzle pieces.

At the school at which I am principal, there are many special projects that introduce values as part of a sound moral education. Third and fourth graders study conflict resolution and are trained to be playground mediators. They explain to 6- and 7-year-olds how to resolve differences by listening carefully to what other people are saying, restating the problem in their own words, and quietly agreeing to solve the problem together. We have class discussions when problems arise and book clubs where values in literature are studied.

We have respect committees, respect banners and skits, and posted Rules for Remembering Respect. These are important parts of the niceness puzzle, but to integrate these and other programs into our school's mission, we as adults have to be consistent in action and deed, from how we respond to one child's excluding another on the playground to issues as broad as service and diversity. Steve Clem, from the National Association of Independent Schools, states, "In schools, moral life is more sea than island."[6] For a climate of niceness to prevail in our schools, we as adults need to address how we treat each other, how we react to others' behavior, how we make decisions, how we deal with disagreements and tensions, how we hold ourselves accountable, how we treat others above and below us on the economic ladder, and how we treat people who are different from us.

Children need real flesh-and-blood role models. They see what we do, how nice or not nice we are, who we hang with and who we don't. When all is said and done, kids aren't going to grow up being nice if they don't see us—mothers and fathers, teachers and principals—acting nice: acting on clear, consistent, and good values. As someone quipped, "Children may close their ears to advice, but they open their eyes to example."

In the end, what I hope for in our school communities is that we honestly can believe it when we say, "You look like a student and I know you're nice"; "You look like a parent and I know you're nice"; "You look like a teacher and I know you're nice." And yes, in deference to my comrades who manage schoolhouses, "You look like a principal, and I know you're nice." Hey, we might as well all be mensches.

December

10

Worry, Be Happy Teachers

This holiday season, this principal contemplates anew a conversation between Sir Thomas More and Rich Richard in Robert Bolt's *A Man for All Seasons*. Sir Thomas More: "Why not be a teacher? You'd be a fine teacher. Perhaps even a great one." Richard: "And if I was, who would know it?" More: "You, your pupils, your friends, God. Not a bad public, that . . . Oh, and a *quiet* life."[1]

Perhaps in Henry VIII's time, that group of four was enough of a public to sustain a teacher. But teachers in today's more complex world appreciate more direct sustenance and respect.

I recently attended an education conference at which the keynote speaker was introduced as "PhD Columbia, BA William and Mary, PS 109 Elementary School." Including one's elementary school in an introduction is a bit corny, perhaps, but it raises a Dangerfieldian question: Do elementary schools get respect?

Sometimes we who educate young children feel like the main characters in *Mike Mulligan and His Steam Shovel*.[2] In this classic children's story, Mike and his steam shovel Mary Anne dig the foundation for the town hall of Popperville and are stranded in the trench they have dug. A little boy comes to their rescue and turns Mary Anne into the town hall furnace, with Mike as the caretaker, restoring these forgotten ones to a place of honor.

We need to respect and honor all of the Mike Mulligans and Mary Annes who dig the foundations of the entire edifice of American education. And so it is that during this holiday season, principals and parents need to thank teachers, who, amid the clamor of educational reforms, reports, reprisals, and reappraisals, lead anything but quiet lives. This gratitude—these "thank yous"—should come from within, not as a result of outside prodding, as our students sometimes require.

Six-year-old Jake had difficulty saying "thank you." I repeatedly met with Jake to rehearse when to say "thank you." I would open my office door for Jake and say, "What do you say?" After much prodding, Jake would finally respond: "Thank you." I would offer a piece of candy to Jake and ask, "What do you say?" After a time, Jake would blurt out, "Thank you," and so it went until Jake returned from a classroom party, favors in hand. "Jake," I asked, "Did you say 'thank you' to your teacher when she gave you your party treats?" "No," Jake asserted, "She didn't ask me 'What do you say?' "

Strange as it may seem, teachers deserve our special thanks (without a coaxed, "What do you say?") because they worry about children. They worry about pushing too much or too little, providing just the right amount of structure and challenge, preparing just the right lesson, reaching each child, meeting all goals, celebrating each child's diversity.

They worry about being sensitive toward children, parents, coteachers, and the teachers next door; they worry about whether parents understand what is going on and whether the kids understand what is going on. They worry about educating children fully for moral as well as academic excellence. They worry about teaching, helping, befriending, cheering, supporting, cajoling, urging, and—yes—loving children.

They worry not just about what they give children, but also about what they take away from them.

Yet most of the time, they go about this strange, beautiful, and demanding profession happily. They turn Bobby McFerron's jazz-pop-feel-good anthem "Don't Worry, Be Happy" on its head. They worry, and they are happy.

Alfred K. LaMotte teaches at the William Penn Charter School. He worries; he is happy. As a part-time clown, juggler, and magician, during the holidays, he, along with his students' help, carries his grin and bag of tricks to this nation's sick and needy. This happy teacher, dressed in his clown outfit, worries as he reflects on his encounter with a very ill child in a hospital room:

The grim silence gets thicker. . . . Then something happens, outrageous and immeasurable. It begins as a soft current rising from the heart, flows up through my throat like a Name with which I am about to name the world. It moves into my jaws and spreads the grease paint on my cheeks: a grin. The grin comes from somewhere deeper than sadness, deeper than sin. It meets the girl's gaze and enters her, as she has entered me. The grin holds. It is real.

Mr. LaMotte offers this advice: "It seems to me that people with a joyful heart make better peacemakers than people with a troubled conscience. . . . To be honest, I think it takes more guts to be happy than to be sad. These days, anyone can be miserable."[3]

Teaching children should be a happy profession. Teaching should also be a worrisome profession. Our schools are blessed with teachers whose happy hearts beat in tandem with worried heads. And this holiday season, this principal is thankful (without being told "What do you say?") for the strange mixture of worry and elation that radiates throughout our school.

11

The Scarsdale Schoolroom

Our culture's obsession with weight loss and educational gain expands the great American waistband as it exposes our nation's educational wasteland, especially during December, and especially for this principal, who gained 8 pounds over the holidays. Unfortunately, in improving learning as in losing weight, common sense is becoming uncommon; we complicate the simple and obfuscate the obvious. You want to lose weight? Eat less and exercise more. You want to learn more? Play less and study harder.

Consider some of the parallels between dieting and learning. During the past two decades, Scarsdale, Atkins, Stillman, NutriSystem, Liquid Protein, and Weight Watchers have become more well-known than Piaget, Bruner, Skinner, cultural literacy, school-based management, assertive discipline, and values clarification. Every year, the diet gurus arrive with an easy way to lose pounds without suffering. Likewise, so-called educational experts delude themselves about the amount of hard work required in schools. Learning, even in the lower grades, may look carefree to those who don't remember. But as somebody once said, it's no accident that teething—one of our first growth experiences—hurts.

Fast-food eating has been translated educationwise into fast-track learning. Nutritional information on diet food packages is more complicated than ever, and there are so many educational buzzwords today that no one really knows what they mean. We suffer from "lite" learning and lean educational fare.

In weight loss, as in educational gain, we think we're better off than we really are. "When it comes to reporting how much we weigh, many of us underestimate either knowingly or not. 'Shaving a few pounds,' writes the *American Journal of Clinical Nutrition*, 'appears to be in the direction of cultural ideals.' "[4] Despite decades of emphasis on new diet foods, reports the U.S. Department of Agriculture, Americans are just as likely to be overweight today as they were in the 1960s.

Participants in the American educational scene suffer from a similar misperception. Of all the studies on schools in the past decade, the most disconcerting one compared 13-year-olds in six countries. Americans placed last in mathematics, but when the students themselves were asked if they were good at math, most Americans said "yes"—the highest positive response of all nationalities. American students recently have scored lower on general achievement tests, but they—along with their parents and teachers—tend to be more satisfied with their performances than are other nationalities.

There are no quick fixes. Fancy health spas with large monthly fees and computer-enhanced, ergonomically designed gadgets cannot take the place of arduous workouts, consistent sweat, and resolve. Likewise, computer-assisted instruction, expensive new textbooks, and multimedia presentations cannot replace long hours of study.

Tommy Tomlinson and Christopher Cross, in an article titled "Student Effort: The Key to Higher Standards," write about the fallacy of effortless learning. "For fear of blaming the victims for their failure to learn," they state, "educators have been loathe to endorse strategies that require hard work from students as a condition for learning."[5] They conclude that, for the past 20 or 30 years, schools and reformers have tried to boost academic achievement without necessarily requiring more effort from the students themselves. In many cases, their reforms made it easier for students to avoid hard work and difficult courses!

Too often, however, it is not only students who don't have to work hard to achieve recognition, but teachers. I recently received an incredible flyer from the Arrid (of Extra-Dry fame) Recognition Program for Teachers. Arrid claims to "believe it is time that credit is given where credit is due." The flyer states (this is true), "For every teacher you wish to receive a special honor roll certificate, just send ten Arrid product proofs of purchase, along with your selected teacher's name, school and grade level to Arrid Teachers Honor Roll, and a personalized honor roll certificate will be mailed back to the teacher." No sweat. Raise your hands, raise your hands! The next award surely will be the Ex-Lax Teacher of the Year! Not a bad idea, actually, as we suffer too much from intellectual constipation; we take in so much and put out so little.

There are, of course, individualized difficulties in weight loss and in learning. Some people have glandular or metabolic problems; learning disabilities are real. But of the weight loss and learning disability experts I have spoken to, all agree that the vast majority of the population needs to do nothing more than eat right and study right.

So let's make it simple and understandable, real and attainable— a New Year's resolution, if you will. Let's eat less and exercise more; let's play around less and study harder. Perhaps by the year 2000, the great American waistband and our nation's educational wasteland will be filled with healthier and wiser Americans.

12

You Don't Eat Jell-O With a Straw

Following in the great tradition of unfulfilled New Year's resolutions, I have found that "Let's eat less" just doesn't cut it with me. I was taught six cardinal rules in Principal's School. Gastronomically speaking, I have violated each one.

Rule 1: *Be a model for your students.* At my first lunch at Sidwell Friends, the first-grade teacher asked me to speak to our 280 children on table manners. Now, you have to understand I was brought up with two older brothers. If I didn't eat my food fast enough, my brothers would eat what was left on my plate after they finished theirs. Unfortunately, my childhood habits of foraging and pillaging have stayed with me. Although the teacher's request left me giggling nervously at the vision of my mother lecturing me on my terrible habits, I did speak to the children on the importance of good manners for minors. I thought I was being at least somewhat effective as a model; that is, until I entered our "cafetorium" and found it sounding like a slew of Slurpies on steroids. Over the din, I heard a second-grade teacher exclaim, "You don't eat Jell-O with a straw!"

Rule 2: *Never criticize or humiliate kids or parents.* It seems that one of our delightful first graders was coaxed into taking a course on children's etiquette by Marjabelle Young Stewart, author of the children's etiquette book *White Gloves and Party Manners.* Everything from drumstick decorum to the art of the ginger ale toast was taught to 13 young children, ending with a highly publicized six-course tea at a fashionable restaurant. When I asked the child (with only a hint of criticism in my voice) in front of her peers and mother why she went to this silver spoon affair, she replied, "The lady in charge wanted us all to be fat and I wanted to be on the news."

Rule 3: *Never rush into decisions.* I have a policy of always tasting goodies made in school to make sure they are edible for our children. A few years back, I walked into a classroom to find delicious smells emanating from the oven. As usual, I opened the oven, looked in, and told the teacher that I wanted a taste. "You'll hate it," she said. "No, I won't," I replied, "Let me have one." I took a bite of what was absolutely the worst thing I've ever tasted. Shortly thereafter, I learned that the first-grade class was raising money for a soup kitchen by baking dog biscuits to sell to parents.

Rule 4: *Never threaten if you can't follow through.* As a neophyte principal, I substituted for lunch duty in a classroom. Melody yelled out, "Somebody took my barbecued potato chips!" I responded to the crisis by violating the first rule of principalship—never make a threat you can't carry out—and said, "No one is going to the lunchroom until whoever took the potato chips confesses!" No one moved. I panicked, and then a stroke of genius hit me. "I want everyone to breathe and I'm going to smell your breath," I shouted. As I came within 10 feet of Michael Harrington, he started to cry, "I took them, I took them! I'm sorry. Please don't call my mom." With that confession and an apology to Melody, Michael and those of us with clean breath went to the lunchroom.

Rule 5: *Never accept food as an excuse.* I received this note from a student sent to my office for misbehaving.

To Mr. Lodish,

I'm sorry I got mad and pushed Jimmy down, but my Mom says I'm hyperactive and I overate too many sweets during lunch and that made me more angry. I'll try to eat less sweets and be better.

From Megan

Rule 6: *Be nice to your teachers.* One of my teachers, a self-proclaimed gourmand, was at my house for dinner with her three kids. Her kids and I went to China Garden to pick up a huge food order and asked for an extra container. We then went to the supermarket and bought a can of dog food and a bottle of soy sauce. In the supermarket parking lot, with a lot of mischievous coaxing from me, her kids and I created a new Chinese delicacy in the take-out box. When we came back, the teacher opened all the containers and re-marked that the one we had concocted "smells unusual, mmm-mmm, let me taste it." She then stopped suddenly in midbite as her daughter, laughing hysterically, raced to the bathroom.

It must be obvious by now that the king of kids (as one child actually called me) can learn a thing or two from the empress of etiquette, Marjabelle Young Stewart, who said, "Dangling food at the end of your fork during a luncheon interview can seriously damage your chance of being hired."[6] Now you know why I've stayed at the same school for 20 years. But at least I don't eat Jell-O with a straw.

January

13

New Year Warranties

This New Year, with all my holiday loot strewn over my living room, I am reminded that I seldom read directions or pay attention to warranties. I fix everything with a hammer.

My new Toro lawn mower breezed through my front yard in 5 minutes. Great job—until my neighbor informed me that my grass was still 4 inches tall. I knew nothing of the newfangled blade disengagement contraption. After I figured out how to engage the blade, I poured 5 pounds of fertilizer into my new Scott spreader, set it at number seven, and pushed it through my front lawn. In 2 minutes and two rows, all of the fertilizer had disappeared. As I explained my problem to a southern gentleman (who sounded like a sheriff talking to the bad guy) on Scott's toll-free 800 number, he said, "Sonny, you done killed your lawn. Ya gots to tighten the screw on the number seven so all the fertilizer don't come a-runnin' out."

Now, I'm not proud of my bumblings. My wife says it's a character flaw. My daughter grits her teeth and smirks. I happen to think that the trait of pushing ahead and learning from one's mistakes corresponds perfectly with being a parent and an elementary school principal.

Children do not come into this world with a lifetime warranty and a "How to Raise Me" instruction manual pinned to their umbilical cords. We all know this too well. That is what makes parenting and teaching so interesting, mysterious, and difficult—especially when our children slide off a predicted or predictable course.

This New Year, I wish I could guarantee all students complete happiness and satisfaction in their lives. I wish I could give all my students a 100% guarantee, as stated in the L.L. Bean catalog: "All of our products are guaranteed to give 100% satisfaction in every way. Return anything purchased from us at any time. If it proves otherwise, we will replace it. . . . We do not want you to have anything from L.L. Bean that is not completely satisfactory." Ah, if life were like that. Dial a toll-free 800 number and get complete satisfaction.

Alas, I can't give any guarantees, but I can at least make a few New Year's resolutions:

1. *I resolve to rid my school and my daughter of pediculus humanus capitis.* My own flesh and blood, with squeaky-clean mop, was lined up outside the nurse's office with 23 classmates. Twenty-two left; one stayed. Danny: "Mr. Lodish, Mr. Lodish, she got it, she got it!" *Kwell. A-200. RID.* Visions of a *Washington Post* headline: "Democratic Head Lice Invade Prestigious School." Head checks—you'd think our school had a resident psychiatrist!

My own daughter was finally sent home from school with the critters, and we were told to wash her hair with medicated RID shampoo. At the neighborhood drug store, my daughter and I waited in a long line to pay for the shampoo. Finally, the lady at the cash register turned to us and, not knowing the price of RID, grabbed her microphone and blasted, "Bill, I need a price for RID. It's for head lice and pubic lice!" At that point, in front of hysterical customers, my daughter collapsed in tears.

2. *I resolve not to mince words.* During the Iraqi war, our school and many others in Washington, DC, received bomb threats. At a meeting of area principals to discuss the situation and find solutions, a colleague exclaimed, "We don't want our kids rushing out at every threat, nor do we want them moving slowly if there is a real threat. What we don't want is a premature evacuation!"

3. *I resolve to help my nephew.* When my nephew first got in trouble, his school counselor asked him who he liked the most. Chaim responded, "God." The counselor then asked, "Well, who do you like second?" Chaim: "Uncle Richie." Perhaps that is why Chaim sent me three citations (this is all true) he received from his junior high school in a 2-month period:

April 9: "This certifies that Chaim Lodish is awarded 'Student of the Month.' "

June 11: "To parent of Chaim Lodish. Subject: suspension notification. Reason for suspension: indecent exposure. Explanation: While waiting for a ride after school on June 11, Chaim pulled down his pants and 'mooned' students in a passing car."

June 16: "This certifies that Chaim Lodish is awarded 'Student Council Award for Good Conduct.' "

4. *I resolve to keep my temper with strangers.* In a heated telephone argument over a school purchase, a representative from an office supply store claimed that we hadn't paid our bill or responded to the store's follow-up letters. She threatened to stop delivery of all future purchases. After a nasty exchange, followed by a non-Quaker period of silence, in which she must have been looking over the name on the invoice, the woman hesitantly asked, "Are you the same Richard Lodish from Cleveland Heights High School who put on the Superman outfit and jumped out of the second-floor window in Mr. Rutan's English class? You are? Well, I'm Claudia Dubin, an old classmate." From then on, it was clear connections with Claudia Dubin, the vendor, and me.

5. *I resolve to destroy or at least hide material confiscated from kids.* A fourth grader came to my office in tears. Mrs. Harker had found five *Playboy* magazines and $10 in his locker. After a mild interrogation, Billy confessed to me that he had taken the magazines from his father's dresser and was selling them for $5 apiece. That afternoon, I interviewed a very straitlaced teacher candidate. I had problems establishing eye contact with her, and I noticed her eyes continually wandered to my open desk drawer. I glanced over at my desk and there was a confiscated *Playboy* centerfold staring at me. Even my detailed explanation didn't quite convince her of my innocence.

6. *I resolve not to let kids swear.* One of our second graders had a problem of cursing in art class. I took him aside and explained that his behavior was inappropriate and disruptive, and I asked him to stop it. I spoke to his mother, who handled the problem in her own way at home, and everyone thought the situation was settled. For a few days, all was quiet in art class—until the day Willie, unable to contain himself any longer, burst out, "Did I hear someone call me an asshole?"

7. *Finally, I resolve to be a vigilant gatekeeper.* While I was in the music room evaluating our music teacher, a tall, attractive gentleman came into the room. As is customary with our many visitors, our engaging music teacher immediately involved him in the students' activities. After a half hour of gyrating and singing to the "Hokey Pokey" and keeping rhythm on a drum to "Little Rabbit Foo Foo," he looked at his watch and reluctantly asked, "Lady, where's the gas meter?"

14

Oil of Delay

Times change. I admire SADD, the organization of Students Against Drunk Driving. They understand that drinking and driving don't mix. Well, I wish they would have told me that drinking and beards and family get-togethers on New Year's Eve don't mix, either. I came to our family gathering in Boston with a 23-year-old beard, gray and distinguished. I left looking like a little *pisher*, or so I thought. My three nephews, who mowed down my beard with only tacit approval from Uncle Richie, said I looked so young I'd get carded at the neighborhood liquor store. Well, I went there with them, noted the large sign by the register, "You must be 21 or over to purchase beer and you must show identification," and bought a six-pack of Michelob. When I politely asked the owner, "Why didn't you card me?" He replied, "I didn't need to." Uncle Richie: "How old do you think I look?" Liquor store owner: "Oh, around 45 or 50."

So my secret is out, or as a third grader innocently quipped, "Your beard looks good off."

Times change. When we're young—like when I began teaching 25 years ago—we want to look older; then when we finally reach some degree of maturity (okay, I said some degree), we want to look young again. Or, as a student remarked to a young-looking older teacher, "You must use Oil of Delay."

But the demarcation between old and young is not so clear. P. L. Travers, the creator of Mary Poppins, once said, "If we're completely honest, not sentimental or nostalgic, we have no idea where childhood ends and maturity begins. It is one unending thread, not a life chopped up into sections, out of touch with one another."[1] Or, as a teacher remarked to our little ones, "Well, kids, I finally grew up and I've been sorry ever since."

Perhaps the best statement about growing up comes from *A Dictionary of Silly Words About Growing Up*: "An adult is a very old child with a huge allowance, easy homework and no bedtime."[2]

But, alas, we can't continually rub in Oil of Delay. We can't delay inevitable aging. But we can understand and support adults as they meander in their own idiosyncratic ways through different phases and stages of adult development.

Various researchers—most importantly, Erik Erikson—have formulated sequential stages of adult development. Erikson charts eight ages of man, later revised by Gail Sheehy and Carol Gilligan to include more of the experiences of women. The three adult stages of Erikson's model are viewed as struggles or turning points: (a) young adulthood, a struggle between intimacy and isolation; (b) middle age, a struggle between generativity, or interest in guiding the next generation, and stagnation; and (c) old age, a struggle to integrate and come to terms with past experience.[3]

In a fascinating book, *Promoting Adult Growth in Schools*,[4] Sarah Levine applies Erikson's and other adult developmental theories to the lives of adults who work in schools. Essentially, her thesis is that because teachers (and administrators) are in different phases of adulthood, they require support appropriately matched to their different developmental needs. For example, young teachers need to cultivate relationships, to experiment, and to learn from mistakes; after years of nurturing their own and others' children, teachers in mid-career need opportunities to develop themselves; and older teachers have generative needs that can be met by sharing school traditions and tricks of the trade with young teachers. Dr. Levine notes that principals especially must attend to adult development "because of the inextricable link between the growth of teachers and the development of students. When teachers stop growing, the learning of their students is hindered."[5]

The incentive for growth must come from within our teachers—from an active need to be intellectually stimulated and to have their horizons expanded. Administrators must be just as concerned about the personal and professional growth of teachers as they are about students.

How does Sidwell Friends Lower School provide for the growth of its faculty? One of the most important, although controversial, ways we encourage growth is by giving teachers a great deal of autonomy in curricular decisions.

Such a policy doesn't mean that our teachers can do whatever they want. The curriculum must be comprehensive and must show continuity. No one argues with that. Basic skills must be taught. No one argues with that, either.

Yet my experience has shown that genuinely good teachers create exciting, well-organized, thoughtful, and challenging classrooms if they have significant responsibility for instructional decisions. According to a veteran teacher at the Lower School, the freedom to teach each child as a true individual leads to teacher growth:

> I feel that the children themselves—that group of individuals so startlingly unique in their differences and similarities—are my primary source for growth. The more children I know and study, the more subtleties of focus and the more variety of subject materials and treatments I can add to the spectrum of my teaching. Resourcefulness provoked by the needs of unique individual problems seems to me the richest source of my growth as a teacher.

A number of organizational structures also promote growth among teachers. One of the most significant and least often acknowledged is team teaching. Frankly, teaching 25 children in a 20-by-20-foot cubicle all day can be a lonely experience. Teacher teams provide a natural setting in which to stimulate ideas, pool resources, and provide suggestions. One Lower School teacher explains the effect:

> Being assigned as team teachers automatically provides opportunities for professional growth. Ideas are shared daily and conflicts arise which, under the right circumstances, can lead to constructive changes.

Our association with neighboring universities has provided another avenue for teacher growth. Each year, many undergraduate students observe and teach in our classrooms. By sharing the nitty-gritty aspects of teaching, then stepping back to explain their ideas and practices to less experienced teachers, our faculty has been prodded to reflect upon and clarify its own teaching skills. From these exchanges, our teachers get the message that their work is valued and that it has an impact beyond their classrooms.

The end result of teacher growth is, of course, its effect on children. When teaching and learning are interesting and exciting to teachers, teaching and learning are exciting to children. When teachers are given the freedom to try new ideas and to take risks, students also feel free to take risks, to learn from mistakes, and to venture into new areas of learning.

All of us in schools must not only respect the sacred time of childhood and the development of our students as they go from lower school to upper school, from little *pishers* to big pushovers, but we must also respect the critical needs that teachers have because of where they fit in the life cycle and how they respond to that fit.

Yes, times change, and even Uncle Richie has passed through more than a couple Eriksonian life stages. But this morning, as I stared at what's left of myself in the mirror with razor and lather in hand, I decided that this would be the last time I pass through Eriksonian life stages whisker-free . . . that is, until I visit my nephews again.

15

A World of Difference

I note the obvious differences
in the human family.
Some of us are serious,
some thrive on comedy.

MAYA ANGELOU
"HUMAN FAMILY"[6]

Given that I thrive on comedy, I often see situations differently than other, more serious members of the human family. When I laugh at something, I am often surprised how sober others seem to be. I imagine that, when they see me giggling, these solemn people might view me as—heaven forbid—not serious enough. Members of my real family often tell me, "That's just not funny."

How do you draw the line between the ridiculous and the somber? It's like the day in late January when my office sink was clogged and I borrowed the custodian's snake to clear it. Churning the snake into the drainpipe—1 foot, 5 feet, 15 feet—I got goosebumps thinking that this klutz was actually clearing a drain all by himself! That is, until I felt a strange sensation on my foot and realized that the snake had forced a hole in the drain pipe and was snaking across my office floor. I laughed; others—including my family—took pity on me.

And then there's my van, which once conked out while my wife and I were on a camping trip. I had it towed to a dealership in a nearby town and, ever frugal (okay, cheap), I convinced the mechanic (and my wife) to let us camp out in the van while it was in the dealership parking lot. All was fine until about 5:00 a.m., when I needed to visit the rest room.

64

As I opened the van door, two huge German shepherd guard dogs almost devoured parts of my anatomy. We then had to huddle in terror, listening to incessant barking and scratching, until we finally were rescued at 8:00 a.m. by the mechanics arriving for work. Was our predicament funny or serious? I guess it depends on your perspective—and the condition of your bladder.

Maya Angelou is correct; there are obvious differences in the human family, but they extend way beyond comedy and seriousness. At our schools, these differences—often very subtle—are played out hundreds of times every day. For example, let's see how different people perceive and interpret a playground tussle between four 6-year-olds.

Teacher A says the kids were just having natural, playful fun; no big thing at all; just part of growing up.

Teacher B disagrees and says one student was taking advantage of smaller children.

Teacher C blames the parents of the aggressive child for being too lenient with him.

Parent A says the kids should learn from the experience; it's a natural, everyday sort of occurrence.

Parent B brings in racial overtones, saying it would have been handled differently if "different kids" were involved.

Parent C says there wasn't adequate supervision.

Parent D says there was too much supervision; the kids should have handled it themselves.

And so it goes. The obvious differences in the human family are played out again and again. The fact is, we all come to the human family—and our schools—with different kinds of intellectual baggage; some of us have it neatly organized, others have all sorts of stuff tossed in and mixed together. We even come with our own lingo-centered baggage. "Underprivileged" to one becomes "overexploited" to another; "multiculturalism" becomes "ethnocentrism."

It's not easy to foresee difficulties before they arise, as my experience with the besieged van can attest, and it can be as difficult to unsnarl a sticky situation as it is to clear a clogged drain. Yet I believe there are ways to bring together the different elements of the human family in our schools and communities.

We need to spend the time to share our perceptions honestly and openly with one another.

We need to keep quiet long enough to not only understand other views, but to appreciate them.

We need to be sensitive (perhaps even oversensitive) to what we perceive as the overreactions of others.

We need to be aware of context—how and why the same brush strokes can paint different pictures.

We need to understand that the more comfortable we become with each other, the easier it will be to share our feelings and reach common ground.

We need to see our world in a mirror, cherishing our own uniqueness and differences, as well as through an open window, learning from and developing a mutual respect for others who are different.

Finally, as we learn to respect differences, we need to appreciate anew our deeper similarities.

Maya Angelou concludes her poem:

I note the obvious differences
between each sort and type,
but we are more alike, my friends,
than we are unalike.

We are more alike, my friends,
than we are unalike.[7]

16

Head and Shoulders

Funny stories are hard to come by in February. Eric Johnson, the noted educator, writes, "To me, teaching is as noble, challenging, stimulating and rewarding a job as one can set one's heart and mind to—except on Fridays and during the month of February."[3]

And so, in February, I spend much time reading and daydreaming—especially, it seems, in the shower. A strange secret I've never before revealed is that, because of my daydreaming, I often lose track of how many times I've washed my hair. I've tried all manner of techniques to curb this tendency to forget. If the top of the Head & Shoulders bottle is off, I've washed it once; if it's on the floor, I've washed it twice; and so on. But nothing works. This morning, I felt my hair metamorphosing into a Brillo pad, my having washed it, I think, some six times.

Lately, in the shower, I've also taken to reading the ingredients listed on my wife's collection of shampoos, conditioners, rinses, and other hair paraphernalia. This is what my morning shower daydreaming has become. (It's similar to my method of catching up on the latest news during breakfast by reading Cap'n Crunch and Cocoa Puffs boxes.) This morning I read the ingredients of Nexus Rejuv-A-Perm: cranesbill, slippery elm, stearic acid, propylene glycol, ergocalciferol . . . sounds like it could not only remove rust from my car, but would also make my fenders smell good. In a throwback to the psychedelic 1960s, it (seriously) "tightens relaxed curls, deepens wave patterns, and renews elasticity." "Definitely a perm's best friend." Far out, huh?

This morning's bout with shampoo ingredients and shampoo forgetfulness has intermingled with my thinking about teacher ingredients and educational forgetfulness.

The most intriguing discussion of the ingredients of a good teacher comes in *Principal Magazine* in an article titled "Good Teaching—The Goosebump Response."[2] Those of us who have had a great teacher or have seen the movies *Stand and Deliver* or *Dead Poets Society* have had the experience of listening to a teacher who is so dynamic that you feel chills go up and down your spine. Surprisingly, although there is disagreement on what constitutes great teaching, there is little disagreement on who the great teachers are. The author goes on to say that teachers who can trigger the goosebump response have, in a sense, mastered the crucial art of teaching. He then relates it to my job: "The sensitive and astute principal will often overlook [other] deficiencies or handle them in a manner that will not jeopardize the goosebump qualities."[3]

My penchant for forgetting how often I shampoo parallels that of educators who forget their own pasts. As someone quipped, "The most enduring quality about education is amnesia."

Educators often get caught in the Bartles & James trap. Baggy pants. Suspenders. Earthy. Straight-talking. We gotta believe 'em. Until we find out that these kindly old fellas were hired by Gallo and are part of a meticulous Madison Avenue marketing plan. Like a Bartles & James ad, educators often succumb to the current media hype for this or that educational trend. Too often, we forget the commonsense elements of what made schools effective in the past.

We forget the balanced approach that good schools have taken for many years. We forget that good teaching is not based on the "radiation theory"—just expose kids and hope they learn—nor is it based on the "carpentry theory"—just hammer knowledge into their heads. We forget that schools need not be so rigid that they limit creativity and individuality, nor so permissive that chaos and confusion reign. We forget what Professor Lillian Katz wisely states, "People think that school has to be either free play or all worksheets. The truth is that neither is enough, there has to be a balance between spontaneous play and teacher-directed work. . . . You have to have the other component—your class has to have intellectual life."[4]

We forget that schools need to turn out more than self-confident kids who don't know anything. As Jerome Bruner has observed,

Let us not confuse ourselves by failing to recognize that there
are two kinds of self-confidence . . . one a trait of personality,
and another that comes from knowledge of a subject. It is of
no particular credit to the educator to help build the first
without building the second. The objective of education is not
the production of self-confident fools.[5]

We forget that when we loosen the curricular reins a bit, when we
risk taking the lid off occasionally, when we encourage creativity and
communication, we can keep the spark and inner spirit of teachers
and students alive.

And we forget "the true form of living, even in school" that Sylvia
Ashton-Warner describes in her intensely moving book *Teacher*, the
story of her 24 years of teaching in New Zealand.

Yet I'm a disciplinarian. It's just that I like the lid off. I like
seeing what's there. I like unpredictability and gaiety and
interesting people, however small, and funny things happening and wild things happening and sweet, and everything
that life is, uncovered. I hate covers of any kind. I like the true
form of living, even in school.[6]

Unfortunately, principals can also forget. I received a letter sum-
moning me for jury duty on 11/5/94. As instructed in the letter, I
called the night before, on December 4th, to get my juror number.
Finding me on her computer, the receptionist started giggling.
"You're an elementary school principal, right?" she asked. "Yes," I
meekly replied. "Well," she laughed, "you were supposed to call last
month on the 4th. The eleventh month is November, not December!
The last elementary school principal we had scheduled for jury duty
got lost in the parking lot!"

Last year, my roommate at an elementary school principals' convention forgot where he had put his dress shoes. Frustrated, he
crawled under the bed and yelled, "I found them! I found them!"
With that, he made a lunge and grabbed my dress shoes, which were
on my feet, nearly knocking me down.

Well, it's back to daydreaming and reading and forgetting in the
shower. Maybe tomorrow I'll just sing in the shower and forget about
the February doldrums.

17

Shoulder Pads

During the February doldrums, a psychiatrist called me for advice. Because he was writing a paper on evaluating psychiatrists, the good doctor wanted to know how I evaluate teachers. Our conversation meandered for 5 days.

On Day 1, I told him that, if I learned anything from my experience as a teacher and principal, it is that good teachers who seek to grow professionally and personally want, need, and indeed should demand constructive feedback. I told him that I have learned that evaluation is a process we do *with* teachers, not *to* teachers.

I told him that feedback to good teachers must be more than a pat on the back for a job well done. I told him that even with the inevitable, natural, and probably healthy anxiety on everyone's part, evaluation can provide much-needed support to teachers. I told him that it can encourage teachers to branch out in different directions, to take risks. I told him that evaluation—with a balance of tact and candor, respect and trust, compassion and honesty—can help teachers grow.

I told him how I go through a lengthy process of conferencing with teachers, spending a day in the classroom, providing feedback, and writing up my comments. I used the up-to-date jargon of clinical and developmental supervision and went on and on. I even shared with him comments made by a Sidwell Friends teacher:

> I think the manner in which we are supervised does a great deal to provide the security in which we can try out methods and talk over our conflicts. The fact that the best is expected

from us, but not within rigid guidelines, gives us just the right mix of circumstances to experiment wisely with topics and strategies. We are prodded and provided suggestions, but in a nurturing, not a demanding, way.

The doctor stopped me abruptly and said, "Look, Lodish, I want the straight scoop. Don't you know what a teacher is like sooner than that?" I thought about it and said, "All right, the truth is—given my experience, so-called expertise, etc.—I could size up most teachers pretty well in 10 minutes. But," I added, "I do feel some guilt about that." "Come on, Lodish," he responded, "your car is going putt-putt-putt-putt-putt. You take it into a gas station; the mechanic opens the hood, and in 10 minutes he says, 'Hey, your carburetor's got some trouble; I'll fix it,' and that's that. What do you feel guilty about? It happens all the time."

That night, I lost sleep wrestling with the car metaphor. Well, on Day 2, I drove into the school parking lot and there was a beat-up 1979 Ford pickup truck with a faded "Boycott South Africa, Not Nicaragua" bumper sticker; a Volvo wagon all neat and tidy with the bumper sticker "The Three Best Things About School Are June, July and August"; a 1976 Chevette with cigarette butts on the floor and the bumper sticker "My Kid Beat Up Your Honor Student"; a 1992 Chevy wagon piled high with old newspapers and McDonald's wrappers; and an immaculate 1993 Buick with Grateful Dead bumper stickers. What our faculty parking lot told me is that our teachers, like their autos, are wonderfully diverse.

Some teachers (and principals) may need an open highway—the more winding the road, the better—others may need directions on how to maneuver on a one-lane country road, and a few may need periodic tune-ups or minor repairs. Similarly, within reasonable boundaries, a supervision system should be flexible enough to accommodate individual teaching styles, to respond to individual teacher needs, and to provide for teachers who want or need to grow professionally in different ways. Yet I do believe—as I told the good doctor that night—there are some "natural teachers" who don't need a lot of bolstering for what they do in classrooms.

After my revelation in the parking lot, I slept fine. Early the next morning, I woke in a daze and had another epiphany after staring at our dresser. Either my wife, who had packed her clothes in a hurry for an out-of-town conference, had cut all her bras in half, or 30 styrofoam yarmulkes attached to velcro were standing on end. I took a few of these to school and asked what they were. They turned out to be shoulder pads. And then I noticed a bulletin board made by a teacher. Mrs. Wilson used her old shoulder pads to make animal figures for a Noah's Ark. I guess there are fads and pads in garb as well as in education.

On Day 3, the good doctor and I had another discussion on how all this and my tendency to sum up someone in 10 minutes relate to hiring new teachers. (Research has shown that decisions are made early in the interview process—often in the first 4 minutes—and are seldom reversed by further information.) Here, I explained my hiring process: culling through hundreds of resumés, interviewing a dozen or so people, bringing back the finalists to teach, having the teachers comment on their teaching, checking all references, and then going through final interviews. And then I admitted that, yes, there are some unpadded natural teacher candidates that come across as outstanding in 10 minutes.

The next morning, I was interviewing what I thought was one of those natural teachers. In the first 10 minutes of the interview, I was impressed by her. I then asked her an innocent question, "Have you ever written student reports on a word processor?" Her response: "I am also a part-time dream counselor. I used to type 105 words per minute, but now I can only type 70 words per minute." "Why is that?" I asked. "Because my finger got caught in a food processor. But every night before I go to bed I visualize it healing and it gets better," she replied, as she wiggled her finger in front of my eyes. "I can even take notes in the dark," she added, "because I am used to waking up and writing down my dreams." So much for first impressions!

On Day 4, I was not able to tell the good doctor about that interview. I had just given a speech on hiring and evaluating teachers at a school outside Philadelphia. A new acquaintance and I received a ride to the 30th Street train station. We were to take the 9:54 p.m. train to Washington. At 9:52, following a brief separation, I was on Track 3 and she wasn't. I said to myself, "She'll get on the wrong train, but I'll miss my train if I go looking for her." So I boarded the train. Twenty minutes into the ride, the conductor requested my ticket and then asked, "Where are you going, sir?" "Me? Washington, DC." In front of 50 riders, the conductor loudly inquired, "What do you do for a living, sir?" A little annoyed, I responded, "I am an elementary school principal." "Well," he chuckled, "that explains it! Son, you're going backwards!" Little kids on the train giggled; older kids applauded. Embarrassed, humiliated, and exhausted, I arrived in New York around midnight.

On Day 5, I made a long-distance call to the good doctor, this time to ask him for advice.

March

18

More Dignity for
Teachers in Films, Please

Teachers need to be accorded more dignity. This came home to me most clearly, after having spent much of spring vacation in front of my VCR.

> I remember the staff at our school. You know, we had a saying—uh—that those who can't do, teach, and those who can't teach, teach gym. And—uh—of course those who couldn't do anything were assigned to our school.

So begins Woody Allen's semiautobiographical romp into his fourth-grade class of 1942 in *Annie Hall*. This scene is part of my videotape collection of every teacher scene that a local video store has to offer. From *Annie Hall* and *Amarcord* to *The Tin Drum* and *Teachers*, my 50 classroom scenes range from believable to bizarre.

I began to assemble my collection 10 years ago, when I was asked to direct a workshop for new teachers. Each year since, I have led discussions on how the vignettes relate to "real" classroom experiences.

Even though I have looked at these tapes again and again, I continue to cringe. Mr. Allen's view of teachers, although entertaining and funny, too often is the way teachers are portrayed on the screen. I'm not talking just about the obvious teen exploitation films, such as *Porky's, Fast Times at Ridgemont High, Breakfast Club,* and *High School,* but also of the many pictures in which teachers in minor roles prance around as bubble-brained, insensitive tuna heads.

76

In *D.A.R.Y.L.*, an arrogant, authoritarian teacher publicly chastises a third grader for cheating, ending his tirade with "Can you imagine what life would be like without ever getting back into my good graces?" In *The Tin Drum*, after failing to stop little Oscar from beating his drum, Miss Spellinhaurer beats a stick across his desk. Oscar lets out a piercing scream, exploding the good teacher's glasses. So much for creative discipline.

In *Teachers*, Mr. Ditto, the recipient of three awards for the most orderly class, dies during one of them. The kids don't even notice. In *Ferris Bueller's Day Off*, the history teacher seems to be taking the day off. Boring and uninvolved, he interrupts his monotone, fill-in-the-blank questions with "Anyone? Anyone?" Then, without a glance upward—and with not one word from a student—he provides the answer. And in *Sixteen Candles*, 16 seconds in an independent study class says it all, as notes—a sex quiz, no less—are passed around. The teacher reads his newspaper and yawns.

In fairness, there are a few exceptions to the predominant portrayal I've described. Movies such as *Breaking Away, Stand and Deliver*, and *The Boy Who Could Fly* show teachers with grace, humor, and conviction. And, of course, there are classics like *Goodbye, Mr. Chips* and *To Sir With Love*, which depict teaching as a way of life. But anyone who owns a VCR will notice that the way teachers have been portrayed in most movies of the past decade shows a lack of respect for this much-maligned profession.

Even when teachers such as Jon Voight in *Conrak* and Robin Williams in *Dead Poets Society* do get respect, they are most often chased out of teaching by inept and uncaring administrators.

I'm not arguing for movies with heroes who miraculously turn gum chewers into class presidents or glue sniffers into honor roll students. Like a mischievous teenager, I get a kick out of seeing an authority figure look ridiculous.

However, the next time Rodney Dangerfield and his cohorts go back to school with camera in tow, I hope they watch Francois Truffaut's *Small Change*, with its sensitive and perceptive portrayal of a teacher in a French village.

When a student is found to be physically abused by his parents, the teacher stands tall and proud in front of his 32 fifth graders and shares with them one of life's great lessons: "I just want to say that because of my own memories, I feel kids deserve a better deal. That's why I chose to become a schoolteacher. Time flies. Before long, you'll have kids of your own. If you love them, they'll love you. If they don't feel you love them, they'll transfer their affection to other people, or other things. That's life. Each of us needs to feel love and to be loved." Even teachers. Even in the movies.

19

Growing Young

"Work and play are two words used to describe the same thing under different conditions." I'm not sure what conditions Mark Twain had in mind when he made this quip, but during the early spring, my thoughts have turned to work and play at school, a place where the twain often meet.

Ashley Montagu, in a fascinating book titled *Growing Young*,[1] explores the concept of neoteny, or the retention into adult life of those human traits—especially play—associated with childhood. From an evolutionary and biological perspective, he argues that we are programmed to remain childlike in many ways; we were never intended to grow "up," but in spirit, feeling, and conduct we are designed to grow *in* and *with* most of the traits that characterize us as children. It's a good thing this book wasn't around when Mrs. Hazelett and my mom were exhorting me to "grow up."

Dr. Montagu cites the recurrent theme of play found in the recollections of many autobiographers from Newton to Darwin. Their description of their work as "play" is no accident, no mere metaphor; they genuinely saw their work as "interesting," "fun," "challenging," and "exciting." This wonderful combination of perceptions and attitudes so characteristic of children (and one found in many school classrooms) is surely not something we are designed to grow out of and certainly not something that we wish to extinguish as we jump-start our youngsters.

Yet play at elementary schools can be controversial, and it forms part of a lengthy educational debate stemming from before the progressive education movement at the turn of the century. The often-quoted dictum of the progressive educator John Dewey, "You learn by doing," did not mean at the time (and does not mean at good elementary schools now) a mindless affair of play. Rather, it means reflective play that enlivens the imagination and stimulates the intellect.

Play at good schools is not simply "fun" (although fun should be part of it); it does not mean making education enjoyable by gutting it and teaching things not worth knowing. There is a huge difference between this kind of play and the joy of learning. All of us who have had a great teacher, or whose child has had a great teacher, or who have seen a great teacher in a movie, know the difference. We also know that learning—real learning—takes hard work, tremendous effort, and time.

In the end, what we wish for in our schools is, in the words of George Bernard Shaw, to see the child playfully "in pursuit of knowledge, not knowledge in pursuit of the child."

And for this principal, one of the key reasons I enjoy my "work" so much is that I am able to keep alive and be in continuous contact with the neotenic behavioral trait of play. I try to relate to kids on their own level, but it doesn't work—their level is higher than mine!

"Hey, Mr. Lodish! You're really weird," exclaimed 6-year-old Jeff as I waltzed with his teacher to the tune *Meet Me in St. Louis, Louie* during our state fair assembly. I thanked Jeff for what I thought was a compliment and, putting my arm around him, said, "You know, Jeff, we're all a little weird, even you." Then, getting into the Mr. Rogers' Neighborhood mode, I added, "But that's good. That's what makes each of us special!" Jeff responded to my rather metaphysical observation by replying, "Yeah, you're special all right; you remind me of that kid who gets in trouble in my class."

Well, Jeff, few of my playful shenanigans match my mischievousness at Halloween—all centered around my motto that it's not Halloween unless I offend someone! Dressed as the Lone Ranger-Sheik, I've led our Halloween parade on a live camel all around our city, until the police chased me and my band of little goblins out of the business district and made me clean up after the camel.

During our head lice epidemic, I began the school Halloween festivities costumed as a life-size bottle of RID. A kindergartner told me I looked like a road sign. One year I dressed as Imelda Marcos and festooned myself with shoes. A first grader commented that I looked like a homeless lady in a shoe store. To commemorate the week our school was without plumbing facilities, I assembled what I thought was a fantastic Halloween costume—the world's first designer jiffy john! I paraded around as the "Spiffy Jiffy—the Benetton Jiffy John," only to have the children tell me that I looked like an ugly robot. One year, I went as Leona Helmsley, poking my head out of a beautifully painted and constructed cardboard hotel and flinging reams of tax forms to my rapt audience. The kids thought I was a crazy lady in a bank. Another Halloween, I garbed myself as a Valley Girl—Gag Me With a Spoon (definitely offensive), and several small students asked me why I'd stuffed two balloons under my wrestler's costume.

Two elections ago, I bedecked myself with "1,000 points of light" (and one dimwit) and marched around tethered to a 200-foot extension cord. Most of the kids thought I was a Christmas tree. Recently, in an effort to appear "politically incorrect," I dressed up as Fidel Castro, propped myself up in an army jeep beside a gigantic bottle of "Castro Oil" red dressing, and dispensed bubble gum cigars to the admiring throng. Most of the kids thought I was costumed as a "big musical instrument." So much for my innovative costumes!

Enough of my neotenic behavioral trait of play. A child must have slipped a "quote pill" into my milk and crackers, for I have to end with one last quote from Nietzsche, who must have had in mind this elementary school principal when he said, "In the true man there is a child concealed—who wants to play."

April

20

April Fools

I t's 8:30 in the morning on April 1, and there in my office is a kind, gentle, salt-of-the-earth teacher of some 25 years, shaking, with tears running down her face. "How can you do this to us?" she yells at me. "This is unconscionable! In all my years at Sidwell Friends School, I've never been so humiliated!" Caught completely off guard, I ask meekly, "Slow down. Tell me what I did that was so wrong." Yanking me over to the faculty mailbox, she pulls out a little plastic cup that had been left—completely unknown to me—in each teacher's box with the following letter dated April 1:

Dear Teachers:

Due to all the concern about drug use across the country, the Administration at Sidwell Friends School has decided that each teacher is to provide a urine sample. Please use the attached plastic cup, put it in the paper bag provided, and give it to me by noon today.

Sincerely,
Richard Lodish

Well, other teachers responded to this note in their own ways. One wise guy came in with a two-gallon plastic jug filled with something. Two angry teachers came in to see me. But most teachers understood that it was an April Fool's joke that turned out to have been orchestrated in secret by two other teachers. Of course, they received huge salary raises, even though I was upset that I had not thought of the prank first.

This rather bizarre episode made me think about how our students question authority. In schools—especially Quaker schools—it is important that students learn to speak out on issues to which they feel a deep, heartfelt commitment. It is also important—as in the April Fool's episode—that they learn to differentiate real from imagined or assumed authority.

This past month, we changed our recess rules and regulations. After a long and healthy faculty meeting about safety and how to help children to become friends and share on the playground, we decided to rearrange the times and areas where children could play certain sports. We thought we were doing the right thing until I received the following "petition" with 50 signatures:

Dear Mr. Lodish:

Mr. Mullin and Mrs. Stevens are making us play soccer when we want to play football. We aren't even excluding anyone. Our parents are paying a good load of money for us to come and have fun as well as learn things. And we don't think it is very fun to be told what to do during recess. Recess is our free time. Please discuss this matter with Mr. Mullin and Mrs. Stevens and please show them this letter. Thank you.

This must all be part of growing up in a democratic Quaker school! The teachers and I held a discussion with these students about what it meant to have a petition, how we would like to have their ideas for recess, and of course we came up with the wonderful idea of the proverbial suggestion box.

A Quaker query adopted by our Board of Trustees speaks to these petitioners and questioners of authority: "Are we teaching our students to be critical thinkers, to move from cocksure ignorance to thoughtful uncertainty?" As our students go from cocksure ignorance to thoughtful uncertainty, they need some help on the way—they don't get there on their own. We need to provide our students with the academic tools and the moral centeredness to be critical thinkers, respectful questioners, and valued community members. In fact, that's the part of our job that makes it so challenging and, well, fun.

On a college tour with my 11th-grade daughter during spring break, I browsed in Brown University's bookstore and discovered a new book—the kind you'd only find in a college bookstore—by Jesse Goodman that provides a context for the above episodes. (My browsing took place after the tour guides comforted anxious parents by announcing, "Hi, I'm Jim and this is Jenny. We'll be your tour guides. We're both juniors and we've been living together for three years!") In *Elementary Schooling for Critical Democracy*, Dr. Goodman argues that the value of individuality in schools must be equally balanced by an ethos of community. Borrowing from John Dewey, Dr. Goodman's radical reform of schooling for democracy seeks to have teachers who help children to "understand the social responsibility that comes with individual freedom and power . . . and to freely examine and express their convictions without fear of intimidation."[1]

Given all this radical university thinking, most Quaker schools do a pretty good job of keeping the teeter-totter of individuality and community, teacher authority and student autonomy, in balance. That is why petitions and even argumentative behavior can be seen not only as students expressing their individual views, but more important, as teachers helping students to learn from their nascent glimpses of democracy and community living.

Until we receive the next petition, I'm glad we came up with the most democratic of solutions, a suggestion box for children's ideas— which, by the way, the kids seem to have forgotten about.

21

Spring Cleaning

Ah, it's tax time, and before being swallowed up by the Sperry UNIVAC 1100/84, I did some spring cleaning. I cleaned my office at work and the office I share with my wife and daughter at home. As I contemplate what I removed from both, I am reminded of what we have kept at our school.

In my office, from my closet door hook and knob, I removed ten foulard and striped ties, three sport jackets, and three sweater-vests. Most days, I leave home outfitted in shirt, tie, and jacket. From home to school, I loosen my tie, carry my jacket, and, when I enter my office, take off my tie and hang it and the jacket on the doorknob. Only on special occasions—perhaps a conference with an upset parent—do I put my uniform back on. (Or, as a Secret Service man quipped to the *Washington Post* a few years back, "If we had a choice, we wouldn't be wearing jackets, but we need them to carry our guns."[2])

Perhaps peeling off layers of clothes on the way to school symbolizes exposing certain trappings found in our schools. Like "The Emperor's New Clothes," we can be fooled by fancy covers, blinded to what's underneath, and embarrassed to discuss what we see and feel. I've seen the spiffiest, best-dressed people make the meanest and nastiest remarks. I've seen wimps in macho clothing. As Marian Wright Edelman, head of the Children's Defense Fund, said, "We give our kids all the things we didn't have and forget to give our children all the things we did have."[3]

To be simple in today's complex schools is a challenge. Yet while simplicity is profoundly important to the texture of life in schools for young children—in schools for all ages—complexity is important, too. Schools need to be joyous places with room for spontaneity, discovery, and humor. When I was in high school speech class, I had to give a speech on a proverb. I chose "Beauty is only skin-deep." I spoke about how trappings aren't important, how we have to look at the soul of a person—all the high school blah blah blah that goes in those speeches. Then I ripped off my shirt, and there on my chest was a wonderfully voluptuous woman painted by my friend, artist Howie Fried. I did receive one of my few *A*s in Speech, but I was sent to Mr. Farenachi for detention and a paddling. I found out that pain, as well as beauty, is only skin deep.

Which brings me to cleaning out our office at home. I began by cleaning out all the educational journals and magazines thrown down and occasionally read. I have often wondered how we educators can fill up thousands of pages each week in these journals and magazines. I wondered, that is, until I looked at the stacks in our office of what are loosely called "women's magazines." Comparisons between women's magazines and educational journals are probably not appropriate, but they're unavoidably tantalizing.

In women's magazines, from *Mademoiselle* to *New Woman* to *Self* to *Cosmopolitan* and *Women's World*, it seems that a large percentage of articles range from "Find Out What Your Lingerie Says About You" to "Sexual Joys: Discover the Pleasures of Being Bad" to "Fitness Move of the Month: Belly Blaster." Educational journals aren't much better, with articles such as "Anatomy of a Top Teacher," "Fertilization and Cleavage in Sea Urchins," and (heaven forbid) "Without Principal: Successful Team Management." (Maybe they found advice in the *Cosmopolitan* article "Fly Like an Eagle Even If You Work for a Turkey.")

Educational ads aren't that bizarre—with a few exceptions. Four different ads from manufacturers to sell a stoplight to control lunch-room noise have now crossed my desk. Green lights give the go-ahead for acceptable sound levels; yellow lights warn of momentary excessive noise, and red lights indicate sustained excessive pandemonium. This automated, sound-operated stoplight sounds like a bio-feedback idea whose time has come. Not only could principals use them in lunchrooms, but we could bring them to room parents' meetings, faculty meetings, and back-to-school nights.

Just last week, I received a brochure with the bold red caption, "All the speeches, letters, and memos you'll ever give . . . already prepared for you."

> Dear Educator: When you're called on to give a speech or write a letter, which is likely to be quite often, do you have enough time? Probably not. Like most school administrators, you almost certainly face never-ending demands on your time. Wouldn't it be great if some or perhaps all of your speech and letter writing had been done for you in advance? It has been. It's available in a remarkable new book. You'll have at your fingertips retirement and testimonial speeches, inspirational speeches, speeches for all holidays, parent meetings, and special events. And you'll have at your fingertips letters to teachers on classroom appearance guidelines, evaluation, student referrals, and personal letters of recommendation.

For only $34.50, my nights at home will no longer be interrupted by the pecking of keys. All my letters of recommendation, nasty letters to parents, and notices of violations of school rules will have been written for the next decade. And I could probably do funerals, bar mitzvahs, and weddings, too.

None of these ads, however, equal the ads in women's magazines for everything from skin-perfecting lotion to microspun powder to cassium gel nail revitalizer with zinc to papaya sculpting spritzer to no-frizz curl freshener to gel cream with liposomes. I still haven't found an ad for what I consider the best of the best—Shalimar perfume. My first real girlfriend wore Shalimar, and I must confess I have a file of the 11 parents on whom I've recognized Shalimar's scent in the past 20 years. I even received a Shalimar-scented letter from a former parent recommending one of her friends for a job. I jokingly mentioned to our food director that I was mailed a perfumed letter. Jack said he had received a perfumed letter, too—in his bill from Macy's.

Well, certain qualities do jump out and attract us. Both educational and women's magazine articles and ads often paint a healthier, richer, more lavish physique or school. When we peel off the layers and get down to what's underneath it all, I am thankful to find myself

at a gentle, caring school imbued with scholastic rigor and integrity.
I'm thankful that I can spend time with our wonderful kids, parents,
and teachers—that is, if I can keep my attire together, my coat jacket
ready when needed, and my eyes on *my* magazines.

22

Mr. Policeman Sir Has Style

Looking rather scruffy in a tasseled cap and torn sweatshirt, I was riding my bicycle near the school where I am principal. The crossing light was red; no cars were around. Out of the corner of my eye, I saw a motorcycle with a policeman on it. Well, I rode the bike across the street. The next thing I heard was a siren wailing. The cop pulled me over and admonished, "You know, it doesn't bother me that you rode across the street on a red light, but you saw me and you still rode across the street. You respect this badge. You respect my uniform."

My response was something like "Sir, Mr. Policeman, sir, Mr. Policeman, sir, I was on a bike, sir." At that point, all 6 feet 2 inches of Mr. Policeman sir asked me for my license. "Mr. Policeman, sir," I replied, "I'm on a bicycle." "You respect this badge. You respect this uniform," repeated Mr. Policeman sir, as he presented me with a $45 ticket and a point on my driver's license. There had to have been many reasons for this juicy confrontation, but I now have figured out that a primary reason must have been the fact that the policeman is an ESTJ, and the bike rider an ENFP. Or, on the Lakota Wheel, he is a northwest while I am a southeast. Let me explain.

Recently, I attended two workshops where participants completed style-type personality inventories. I won't bore you with details, but we were asked to answer questions such as, "I let other people control my actions. (1) usually, (2) often, (3) sometimes, (4) occasionally, (5) rarely, (6) never." These responses were then tallied on a grid and participants categorized into different types. On the

Myers-Briggs Type Indicator, I am an ENFP, which stands for extroversion, intuition, feeling, and perception, which, loosely translated, means that I am assumed to be warmly enthusiastic, a planner of change, imaginative, and individualistic, and that I pursue inspiration with impulsive energy, seek to understand, and inspire others. And I'm just guessing the good policeman had to have been an ESTJ—fact-minded, aggressive, analytic, systematic, more interested in getting the job done than in people's feelings.

At a Leadership Washington meeting, where so-called leaders from metropolitan Washington get together, we formed what the consultant called a Lakota Medicine Wheel. Each of the members, from CEOs to lawyers to heads of service organizations, scooted to one of four quadrants according to how each of us felt we related to others: north being assertive, active, decisive; south being supportive and nurturing; east, visionary; and west, analytic. Well, 40 people got into about a half-dozen different zones and began to argue over why they preferred the area they had chosen. But in the end, all these leaders concluded—almost like the end of a fairy tale—that all types have to work together and understand each other to get ahead and get along. Yes, even northwest policemen and southeast principals.

As a result of these two workshops, it became obvious to me that if adults have such distinct styles and types, then it seems reasonable to conclude that our students also have their own approaches to other people and, ultimately, to learning.

In fact, a lot has been written on teaching styles and learning styles. Robert Sternberg, the IBM professor of psychology and education at Yale University, has devised intriguing methods to enhance learning by better understanding and aligning teaching and learning styles. Describing a style as a "preferred way of using one's abilities," Dr. Sternberg says that styles are not inherently good or bad; they're only different.[4] In a compelling theory, he compares teaching and learning styles to the organization and function of governments (a theory known as mental self-government). For example, in education, a liberal would be a child or teacher who likes to do things in new ways and defies convention, whereas a conservative learner or teacher likes to do things in tried-and-true ways and follows convention. A monarchic learner or teacher likes to do one thing at a time, whereas an anarchic takes a random approach to problems and dislikes systems and constraints. A legislative person likes to create and invent; judicial people like to judge and evaluate.

Dr. Sternberg argues persuasively that students do better when their styles resemble more closely those of their teachers. A teacher who is monarchic and likes to do one thing at a time may go crazy with an anarchic student, who jumps into several projects randomly. Teachers need to help these students direct their energy in an organized and focused way. Conversely, a teacher using traditional methods would benefit children with an executive and conservative style, who follow directions and do what they're told. Students with these styles need to learn to take risks and venture into new areas of learning. Neither teaching method is uniquely correct. The key is to vary approaches. As Dr. Sternberg states, "Teachers must accommodate an array of thinking and learning styles, systematically varying teaching and assessment methods to reach every student. The key is variety and flexibility, using the full range of styles available."[5]

My experience has shown that great teachers develop an intuitive sense for aligning their teaching methods with the many styles in which kids learn. Although schools may put different rubrics on style alignment—such as individualized instruction, customized learning, challenging children with different levels, and meeting the needs of students—achieving an appropriate match with every student is, in essence, what our schools should be about.

And so, my friend Mr. Policeman sir may not have been the best match for this student, but I'm sure that, after sufficient training with Dr. Sternberg, his judicial, monarchic, internal conservative style would become more compatible with my global, external, liberal, anarchic whatever. Then, the next time this ESTJ encounters an ENFP, Mr. Policeman sir will align his straitlaced policeman style with the culprit's laissez-faire bicycle style and let him off without even a warning.

P.S. After a court hearing, the judge reduced the $45 fine and a point to a $25 fine and no point. *Dum da dum dum, dum da dum dum duuummm.*

May

23

Casting for Kids

Spring is also a time for fishing. As a devoted fisherman, I see a similarity between fishing and teaching. There is a story about a teacher who took his students ice fishing. As they started to cut a hole in the ice in which to drop some worms, a booming voice said, "There are no fish there!" The group moved about 20 feet away and began to cut another hole in the ice; again the voice exclaimed loudly, "There are no fish there, either!" The teacher looked around and yelled, "Who are you and how do you know there are no fish there?" The voice replied, "I'm the owner of the ice-skating rink."

The sad truth today is that, even on a freshly thawed pond stocked with bass, many fishermen approach fishing with limited vision. Similarly, in a school stocked with kids, many teachers approach teaching as if they are wearing blinders.

The fishing-teaching metaphor is particularly significant today, for it emphasizes the central dynamic that is missing from our proposed national agenda of educational standards, tests, and school report cards, and what, it seems to me, is the central problem: what happens between pupil and teacher. The fishing-teaching metaphor also parallels my own fishing-teaching career and provides me with insight into why we have fishermen—and teachers—of varied effectiveness and talent.

As a novice fisherman, I did as Uncle Benny showed me. I put a worm on a hook, simply cast it out, let it lie on the bottom, and waited for a fish with an appetite. Over the years, through trial and error and seeing what the guy fishing next to me did, I refined this technique. I used different rigs, weights, hooks, rods, and reels. I even learned to give the fish time to swallow the bait before striking. Mostly, though, I learned that bait fishing is essentially fisherman centered; we wait for the fish to come to the bait.

Like bait fishing, most teaching today is teacher centered. We cast out some knowledge, we present a lesson, and wait. Then we expect kids to get hooked on learning. As with fishing, some teachers have perfected this technique; they know what strikes and when; they know when to cast out and when to pull in. But, like many bait fishermen who lack experience in other fishing methods, many teachers aren't aware that there are different, more exciting ways to teach. Even though a lot of kids may swallow their presentations, these teachers miss the excitement, engagement, sensitivity, and interaction between themselves and the children.

I fished with bait for years and taught in this manner as a beginning teacher. Then, later in my teaching career, I met Chuck of Chuck's Tackle Shop. He hooked me (spiritually and emotionally) on fly fishing and, quite by accident, helped provide me with a clearer vision of the nature of exceptional teachers. On rivers and in schools, I learned to appreciate and understand the aesthetic, the elegant, the natural.

Fishing became an active, creative type of angling, drawing on alert senses and self-control. I learned that fly fishing must be cultivated and pursued as an art, yet I also learned that I must approach it with scientific dedication and thoroughness. Most important, I learned that there was a need to know how—softly and cautiously, yet with confidence and finesse—to cast out the right fly with flowing elegance. I found that it takes incredible preparation, practice, and patience. Once I was hooked, I never experienced a similar thrill from other methods of angling nor viewed the aquatic world through the same eyes. I discovered that fly fishing is ultimately fish centered. The fisherman freely and passionately goes to the fish.

Likewise, I have learned that great teaching is ultimately child centered. I have learned that superb teachers engage, communicate with, and truly tie in to each student's learning. With a sense of assuredness that comes from preparation, experience, and expertise, great teachers meet the natural rhythm of children and teach in harmony with the children's development and habitat. They know when to instruct, guide, and lend a helping hand as their students are lured into the excitement and challenge of learning. Ultimately, there is a spiritual bonding. Yet great child-centered teaching—like fly fishing—is also playful and exhilarating, filled with infinite variations.

Many more fishing-teaching parallels can be drawn. The nearly confessional autobiographies of fly fishermen have a fervor, sentimentality, and inspiration similar to the personal diaries of progressive teachers who have challenged traditional methods. Both fly fishing and child-centered teaching have been mistakenly surrounded by an aura of exclusiveness and complexity. But I'll let the metaphors rest.

To begin a true "renaissance in American education," I suggest that all the educational bigwigs go on a REAL fishing trip. As for me, it's a nice spring day—I think I'll get some rods and reels and take a few teachers over to the lake and go ice-skating.

24

Correcting Educational Presbyopia

Not having seen as much as I would like to have seen this school year, I finally broke down and bought bifocals. Well, sort of. For the past year, I have had a prescription in my wallet to correct my "presbyopia"—the natural stiffening of the crystalline lens of the eye, which occurs in virtually everyone in their forties. I was experiencing great difficulty in focusing on close objects as well as seeing distant ones clearly. Now, with my new Varilux Infinity No-line Bifocals, not only can I see clearly near and far, but I now have "lineless natural vision." According to the Varilux literature, this makes it "easy to switch viewing between distance and up close without a visible dividing line between the two."

If only educators could view students with bifocals like these. Instead of the natural hardening of the eye's crystalline lens, many educators suffer from a natural hardening of perspective. We either get so involved with focusing on short-term learning that we lose sight of more distant goals, or we get so involved with clarifying long-term objectives that close-up learning is neglected.

To what end do we educate kids today? And to what degree should the distant dictate the near? Should the year 2000, the competitive marketplace, and the global economy affect what happens in our classrooms? Or should schools concern themselves with the here and now of experiential learning—learning for its own sake?

Two renowned educators have looked at educational presbyopia—one 70 years ago, one recently. John Dewey often has been misunderstood for his supposedly short-sighted support of child-

99

centered education driven by children's natural impulses. But as a new book by Robert Westbrook, *John Dewey and American Democracy*, makes clear, Dewey was convinced that the true teacher must discover the steps that intervene between the child's present experience and his or her richer maturity. Dewey insisted that, for education to have meaning, it must extend a child's curiosity and interest to more distant knowledge embodied in subject matter.[1]

In *The Unschooled Mind: How Children Think and How Schools Should Teach*, Howard Gardner states his belief that because educators misinterpret the near, they cannot adequately focus on the far. He argues that many students, unbeknownst to their teachers, "continue to be strongly affected by the practices, beliefs, and understanding of the five-year old."[2] As an example, he suggests that if you ask a 5-year-old why it is hot in summer, he or she will probably say it's because the earth is closer to the sun. Unfortunately, many high school seniors will have the same response.

As for me, I remember as a child being labeled a "war baby" by my parents. Until the age of 9, I thought that meant I was born under a covered wagon with cowboys shooting bullets and Indians slinging arrows above me. During this same stage of arrested development, I overheard my dad complaining to my mom about my older brother's orthodontia, "Darn it, Syl, the kid's got a new car in his mouth." For years, I looked for the fins and tailpipe to emerge amidst the silver crackle of my brother's braces.

Gardner believes that instead of challenging and building on children's real understandings, many schools simply ignore them and proceed to fill their minds with new and distant information. Only when teachers acknowledge and build on the assumptions made by the 5-year-old mind, Gardner argues, will students internalize the lessons taught in school and be able to apply them outside the classroom.[3]

When explaining why it's hot in summer, what war babies are, or the high cost of orthodontia, teachers need to wear bifocals in order to engage students in real understanding while providing them with the tools to be lifelong learners. Up close, we want to do things right; looking into the distance, we want to do the right thing.

But even bifocals can play strange tricks on you. There is a story of a young man who lost his keys late at night at our school. George, the diligent night watchman, found him looking for his keys—

bifocals and all—under a light in front of the building. George: "Where did you lose your keys?" Young man: "In the parking lot." George: "Then why are you looking here?" Young man: "Because the lights in the parking lot are turned off." Proper illumination and proper bifocals don't necessarily lead to proper conclusions. Even with my impressive new glasses, I still was struck by the directions I found in the packet in front of me on a recent airline flight: "If you are sitting in an exit row and you cannot read this card or cannot see well enough to follow these instructions, please tell a crew member."

In the whimsical children's story *The Shrinking of Treehorn*, little Treehorn, who is shrinking, is sent to see the principal—a man obviously in need of bifocals:

> When the lady said he could see the Principal, Treehorn went into the Principal's office with his form. The Principal looked at the form, and then he looked at Treehorn. Then he looked at the form again.
>
> "I can't read this," said the Principal. "It looks like SHIRKING. You're not SHIRKING, are you, Treehorn? We can't have any shirkers here, you know. We're a team, and we all have to do our very best."
>
> "It says SHRINKING," said Treehorn. "I'm shrinking."
>
> "Shrinking, eh?" said the Principal. "Well, now, I'm very sorry to hear that, Treehorn. You were right to come to me. That's what I'm here for. To guide. Not to punish, but to guide. To guide all the members of my team. To solve all their problems."
>
> "But I don't have any problems," said Treehorn. "I'm just shrinking."
>
> "Well, I want you to know I'm right here when you need me, Treehorn," said the Principal, "and I'm glad I was here to help you. A team is only as good as its coach, eh?"
>
> The Principal stood up. "Goodbye, Treehorn. If you have any more problems, come straight to me, and I'll help you again. A problem isn't a problem once it's solved, right?"[4]

Right! Maybe after all, the real trick for teachers and principals is to see the unseeable. I think the fox in Saint-Exupéry's *The Little Prince* knew something when he shared his "very simple secret" with the Little Prince. He said, "It is only with the heart that one can see rightly; what is essential is invisible to the eye."[5]

June

25

Educational Elisions

Now that the school year is officially over, I can envision with my new bifocals not only what we accomplished this year, but also what we omitted. In education, the latter is often more important than the former.

> ... A region at the front of the organ controls sexual function, and is somewhat larger in males than in females. But its size need not remain constant. Studies ... by Stanford University neurobiologist Russell Fernald reveal that certain cells in this tiny region of the brain swell markedly in an individual male whenever he comes to dominate a school. Unfortunately ... the cells will also shrink if he loses control of his harem to another male.[1]

Before you all get upset, let me tell you that the above quote was in *Time* magazine. And when we fill in the ellipses (. . .), the quote takes on a different meaning. The first omission, or elision, is "in animals"; the second is "of tropical fish," and the last is "for the piscine pasha."

Well, at least piscine pashas don't dominate real schools (or control real harems). But when I think of the real people who do control and dominate schools, I see them too often substituting their own misleading actions and theories for the elisions that have been made from education. Too often, they forget what teaching and learning and childhood are all about. I have three suggestions to help these elision makers:

1. *Administrators need to get into real classrooms and teach.* A recent article in the *Montgomery Journal* titled "Desk Jockeys Brace for Class"[2] describes how, to save more than $115,000, Montgomery County public school administrators have been asked to return to classrooms to substitute. A staffing specialist was quoted as claiming, "It's a kind of thing that no one really believes is a great idea." I think otherwise. The "desk jockey" substitutes will cover 1,450 days this semester. This fiscal necessity should lead to better policy, provide reality checks, and help fill in and provide perspective on real elisions being made in classrooms.

2. *Educators need to be learners themselves.* John Holt, author of *How Children Learn* and *How Children Fail* and 11 other books, was a writer and teacher who came to public attention as a leading critic of the American school system in the 1960s and 1970s. Believing that he could not write about learning without being actively engaged in it himself, John Holt took up the cello at age 40 and devoted much time to becoming a skilled player. In his book *Never Too Late*,[3] published in 1978, he wrote about the exhilarating experience of learning something new so late in life.

Well, at the same point in life, I tried to learn to play the harmonica and signed up for a Montgomery County extension course. Every type of *Homo sapiens* was in the course—a farmer, a lawyer, a businessman, a teenager, a shoe shiner—25 of us, all taught by a guy named Slim who worked at a supermarket as a bagger and played blues harmonica at night. It was a beginner's course, and we all started at the same level. "Harmonica Lodi" never got too far; I ended up buying *Harmonica for the Musically Hopeless*, a $3.95 book on the level of a second-grade workbook (kind of a *Cliff's Notes* for harmonica) that had little cards with numbers and arrows going up and down to correspond to notes on the harmonica. Number three up, you'd blow on Hole 3; seven down and you'd draw on Hole 7.

I took the course 1 day a week for 4 months. On the last day, we had a performance. I played "Row, Row, Row Your Boat." With dry lips and trembling hands, I got through it with some minor applause and only a couple of giggles from the youngsters in the back. From this course, I learned that a little tenderness and good humor from the instructor could be sufficient encouragement. I saw from a new perspective the highs and lows of learning. And because of a few respectful pats on the back from Slim and fellow students, I was never humiliated, even when the 9-year-old played "Amazing Grace," bending all the blues notes that I could never bend. But I also learned that the closest God came to giving "Harmonica Lodi" musical genes was a Walkman tucked in the pocket of my Levi's. I still keep that harmonica in my desk and play it—mostly when no one else is around—an elision in deference to music lovers with which few would argue.

3. *Educators and policymakers need to see children as they really are.* The kindergarten at Abington Friends, a wonderful Quaker institution outside of Philadelphia, has been termed "The School of Soft Knocks" by *People Weekly* magazine,[4] and it offers "Back to Nurture," a kindergarten for grownups taught by Betsy Smith. For $30 on Saturdays, psychiatrists, attorneys, homemakers, and writers gather in her classroom to revel in 3½ hours of "unadulterated childhood." "It's nice to be able to do whatever you want and not be judged by it. It's a place that's safe and you're encouraged to be who you are," says one of the participants. Steven Spielberg describes childhood as "that feeling of safety when you could make a mistake, but not be held accountable for it—a feeling of being home and protected."[5] Viewed in a Spielbergian way, childhood is warm milk and cookies.

Yet educators and policymakers need to learn about the whole reality of childhood—including the part that's not warm milk and cookies: the school of hard knocks. They need to look at the real elisions that are forced on children in this country. Scores of government and foundation committees, as well as the Children's Defense Fund, report that child deprivation has increased. One of every four U.S. infants and toddlers lives in poverty; there are 13 million children with no health insurance; and the United States ranks only 19th among nations in preventing infant mortality. The list goes on and on. We need to put aside political divisiveness and misconceptions and push ourselves and our leaders to help ensure the health, safety, and education of all of our children. Our families urgently need our help. Perhaps the American family is the most imperiled institution of all. Real elisions need to be filled for far too many of our nation's children and families.

Filling in these elisions will not be accomplished by the rhetoric of desk jockeys, but by policymakers, administrators, teachers, and parents learning anew and working together for the benefit of children. With all these elisions from education, however, it's probably just as well that only piscine pashas dominate schools because the good and strong teachers of my school would never allow swelling in the tiny dominator region of "Harmonica Lodi's" brain.

26

Nostalgia

The end of the school year is a time for nostalgia and is probably as good a time as any to come clean with one of my few passions and fascinations: school collectibles of the past. There are reasons for my madness; my interest in antique "school things" has given me an intimate look at exactly what students carried to school, what students did there, and what items the marms and masters once used to conduct their classes. I feel a special kinship to my old school things, and I see this collecting as a natural adjunct to my profession.

My offices at school and home are cluttered with old ABC blocks, slates, pencil boxes, ABC boards, handwrought books from the early 1800s, schoolgirl maps, rewards of merit, old school desks, ABC puzzles, old report cards, wooden crayon and chalk boxes, kindergarten blocks, sewing cards, number frames, and needlework samplers. My collection goes on and on. I've been known to drive 200 miles to an auction for an alphabet board, and I correspond with people around the country about their school collections. I covet few things, but these items are the fabric of my trade, and they do provide a common thread with schools of the past.

But all of them are mere things. When I look at my alphabet boards or my 1880 kindergarten blocks, my mind wanders to the child who played with these learning tools and what thoughts this child had. What was the little 8-year-old girl thinking when she spent 2 months tediously working on an ABC sampler? Or the 9-year-old boy who in 1845 copied 100 times, "Even from learning springs most noble things?"

When I look at all my old school stuff, I am also reminded that today's educational trends are the product of a long history, and I can't help daydreaming about the schools of the future. What will be hammered down at auction from the archives of my school in the year 2095? Will it be fourth-grade books in the back of the library—hand-bound no less—written for our first graders? Perhaps the Friday morning play programs that our children put together? What about the "Celebrating Diversity" banner hanging in the hall? The posted Queries? The bird books of our first graders? Videotapes of our assemblies? Who knows, maybe a computer printout of our test scores? Maybe the combs used to check for head lice. Or will there be calculators, CD-ROMs, laser disks, or computer simulations designed by our children? In the year 2095, will teaching and learning be that different? Will all the bells and whistles of technology dramatically change what will happen in our classrooms?

And, for that matter, who understands fully the day-to-day, minute-by-minute reality of our classrooms? What artifact could capture what really occurs in our Lower School today? How could we frame the anxiety and the joy of our first graders when books and words begin to take on a magic of their own? How would we show the close and lasting friendships that have developed? What school memorabilia would describe the time one of our students felt on top of the world, and the time when she felt that nobody liked her? What item could impart the moment when a second grader understood that learning requires hard work and concentration, when he learned that he may not always be first, second, or even third in all that he does? What school collectible could capture the moment of magic and joy when a kindergartner creates something special and unique with her hands, her voice, or a musical instrument?

What relic would we use to describe a clique of boys and girls on our playing fields arguing and then making up? What school artifact would we use to describe the sense of pride and accomplishment when a 4-year-old cuts a carrot with an older student during our Wednesday morning service program? What antique-to-be would show the struggle that went into finishing a research project on Egyptian mummies, the composition of a Japanese haiku, or a math pattern represented by contorted bodies? What items would show a student's newfound sense of independence and competence? What collection of school things could possibly demonstrate how our students' personalities have been framed and are imprinted on who they are and who they will become?

Perhaps a hundred years from now, a principal, full of nostalgia, reclining on some newfangled chair and looking through school artifacts from our time, will allow his mind to wander as my mind has wandered. Perhaps she'll have a new and better view of learning, teaching, and education. But my guess is, after all of our old stuff is examined, the same moments of engagement, frustration, effort, anxiety, joy, magic, peace of mind, pride, struggle, and dreams will exist. My guess is that, underneath all the educational trappings, the marms, masters, and kids in the class of 2095 will not be all that different from those in the class of 1995.

July

27

Fit to Be Tied*

I have always thought it a bit incongruous during summer vacation to be reading a classic while propped up on a beach chair with sand castles everywhere, frisbees flying, boom boxes blaring, and children and Diet Pepsi cans strewn about. Presently immersed in *Anna Karenina*, I can only guess how Count Leo Tolstoy would have taken to a school principal savoring his great novel in such surroundings.

Tolstoy himself was a principal of sorts. During the 1860s, he founded an experimental, highly romantic, and quite permissive school for peasant children on his estate, Yasnaya-Polyana. Tolstoy, in an essay sketching the character of his school, boldly commented, "Like all living beings, the school not only becomes modified with every year, day, and hour, but also is subject to temporary crises, hardships, ailments, and evil moods."[1]

Schools—like all living beings—have had and will continue to have their share of temporary crises, ailments, and evil moods. As an example, I offer this cautionary tale.

For as long as there have been schools and principals, it has been obvious to everyone over the age of 4 that the principal's office is a place where you go when you are in trouble. A related truth is that the principal's office is a place where principals too can get into trouble. In fact, it's very easy to get into trouble in the principal's office if you are the principal.

*Coauthored by Richard Lodish and Nick Thacher. Originally published in *Principal* magazine, January 1990.

Last summer, Nick Thacher, head of an elementary school in Connecticut, found himself in his customary ruminative state, trying to decide what to write for his first parents' newsletter. What could be said about the start of the school that hadn't already been said thousands of times?

Realizing that Velcro straps had virtually replaced laces on children's shoes and that the first written communication of the year is often the only one that is read carefully, he wrote the following tongue-in-cheek missive:

> At last the children will return and we look for the most significant harbinger of our new year. The true megatrend is quickly revealed: *Velcro straps for shoes.* At the risk of stretching the idea a bit, I offer a few reflections . . . we might call "shoestrap elaborations."

> Prepare, as always, to wrestle with the ancient issue of peer pressure. We are used to comparisons of bedtime hours, the sizes of allowances or Garfield dolls, the relative programming capacities of microcomputers. But how come I have to have shoes with laces, when all of my friends have Velcro straps?

> Reflect, for a moment, on what I call The Virtue of Hard Work. How can we best transmit it to our children in the face of a narcissistic culture? Do we make their lives too easy? That quick strap may epitomize a new reality that demands our consideration (even if we do wear loafers ourselves!).

> I offer several points of merit for those enraging, dragging laces:

> 1. Mastery of a task—it is hard (remember?) to learn to tie shoelaces.
> 2. Development of small motor skills—I can hear the lament of the early elementary teacher, "We're already confronted by children who have been given a pencil too early and learned the way not to hold it!"
> 3. Enriching interaction between parent and child—our lives are frenetic, I know, but we mustn't move so quickly that

we overlook these special opportunities for helping, sharing, growing, and accomplishing: "Here, let me help you
with your laces," and "Look, I've learned to do it by myself!"

This seemingly innocuous piece ignited a parental firestorm. The
principal had forgotten how much trouble one could get into without
setting foot outside the principal's office. He had forgotten how much
scrutiny his words would bear from anxious parents. The phone
began to ring . . . and ring: Should I get my child new shoes? What is
wrong with parental convenience? What sort of an antiquated value
system is operating in your school?

As most school brouhahas do, this one eventually subsided. (The
children, of course, were only minimally aware of the silliness.) And
there the matter might have rested, had not Thacher innocently related his Shoestrap Saga to me, who in turn retold the story to a small
group of parents.

An unidentified informant leaked bits and pieces of those remarks to the press and the following item soon appeared in the
Washingtonian magazine:

Teachers at The Sidwell Friends School have been quietly
asking parents not to outfit their children with Velcro-fastened tennis shoes. It seems that the sound of repeatedly
ripping Velcro has been shattering the atmosphere of calm
reflection in Quaker meetings.[2]

In the wake of the subsequent hullabaloo at Sidwell Friends, I
saw no alternative but to clear the air once and for all by revealing The
Truth to the magazine's readers. In the next issue, the *Washingtonian*
printed my letter:

As a principal . . . I have learned that what you need to keep
things tied together and to keep yourself from getting booted
out is to have parents hold meetings around meaningless
issues. . . . With this administrative principle in mind, I admit
. . . I told a story to a group of Sidwell Friends parents about
a principal friend of mine who wrote a letter to his parent
body on the perils of Velcro. Little ones, he wrote, never learn
how to tie their shoes. Well . . . parents held special meetings

and wrote long letters. For a year, no one complained about teachers or curriculum. No one even complained about school lunches. Did Velcro really lead to physical and moral impairment? Or, as others held, did Velcro's virtues—ease of use for both children and parents; no more tripping over untied laces—matter more? The controversy raged, while other issues went unnoticed for the duration.[3]

But there's more. After the news item appeared, I received a comradely note from a reader in Michigan:

As a just-retired teacher of twenty-nine years, I have to tell you how I solved the problem [of noisy Velcro shoes]. I told the children that when they fooled with the shoe, I had to take it, and I always did. They walked around all day without it and got it back when they went home. . . . The problem totally disappeared. Hope this helps you.

And so our cautionary tale of woe ends with neither a bang nor a whimper. But in two schools, the muffled sounds of Velcro straps being ripped apart are a subtle, yet constant reminder that trouble never treads far from the principal's office—especially if you're the principal.

28

Tennis Rules

I wanted to learn how to play tennis, so I did what many aspiring tennis players do. I bought a T-shirt with a little alligator on it, pants with a little polo player on them, Reebok tennis shoes, tennis socks, a tennis cap, and a brand new tennis racquet. I got up Sunday morning for a tennis game, put on most of my spiffy new duds, and walked around the corner to the tennis courts. I got there and was all set to go when I glanced down and saw that I'd forgotten to put on my tennis shorts. I ran back home in my underwear and, well, the rest is history.

During the summer, I still play tennis and still work in my office. The percentage of time I spend on each, though, depends on who is asking the question. If a fellow administrator asks me for a document, I say, "Oh, I'll try to get it to you, but I have too much to do in my office. I'll be busy for the next three hours." If, however, a fellow tennis hacker calls for a game, I'll immediately respond, "Sure, I've got nothing better to do. I'll be there in 10 minutes."

Now I'm what you call an ordinary tennis player—maybe fair to middlin' would be more accurate. In dividing my time between school ruckus and tennis racquets, this ordinary player has seen a great deal of similarity in how tennis players and students behave in ordinary situations. Both groups, it seems to me, need explicit guidance on how to behave. Tennis players must know not just the rules of the game, but how to play the game—with courtesy, few temper tantrums, and remembering that the goal is to have fun. Likewise, in school, students need to understand not only the rules of what is prohibited, but how to play and work—with courtesy, honesty, responsibility, kindness, respect, and few temper tantrums.

Unfortunately, not enough guidance is given on the courts or in classrooms. We expect tradition and custom to be readily understood when, in fact, we need to provide and model explicit behaviors. There are dozens of magazines and hundreds of books on tennis strokes, techniques, and tactics, but almost nothing on how to handle oneself on the tennis court. Whereas schools have all sorts of rules and regulations, often we do not pay enough attention or offer enough guidance to make sure children actually put into practice what we stand for and believe in.

An example from the world of tennis: In a 164-page book of rules, regulations, violations, and officiating techniques from the U.S. Tennis Association, the following cryptic message is found in a tiny appendix: "There are a number of things not specifically set forth in the rules that are covered by custom and tradition only." Several procedures that players should use to get along on the courts are listed: Don't shout loudly or have a postmortem on each point to the dismay of the players on adjoining courts; don't sulk when you are losing, instead praise your opponent's good shots; and "Above all, try to make tennis a fun game."[4]

By playing and closely watching tennis this summer—when I'm not in my office, of course—I have concluded that we also need a behavior code for our school rules. We must strive to make more concrete and visible—showing by example—the often informal and taken-for-granted modes of behavior that help us get along and respect one another.

"Violations" of good behavior on the courts and in the classrooms have led me to this conclusion. Similar examples of bad behavior exist in our schools and on our courts:

1. *Blaming the other guys.* After receiving an easy serve on the court next to me, a player hit the ball directly into the net and yelled, "Darn it, I can't get any pace with that dinky serve. What a lucky hit on your part!"

Similarly, at school, I recently received a letter blaming another child for the writer's aberrant behavior: "Dear Mr. Lodish, I'm sorry I threw spitballs in the boys' bathroom. I don't mean to be making accusations, but it never would have happened if Daniel hadn't told me how to. I admit I have tried before, but if Daniel hadn't told me how, it never would have worked and I would have left. I have only one more thing to say. I came initially to the bathroom because I wanted to see Teddy's cut, because he was just then taking a bandage off his head."

2. *Blaming outside forces.* I played tennis with a guy named Chip a couple of weeks ago. After Chip lost the first set, he started comparing Wilson tennis balls to Dunlops, saying the reason he lost was that the Wilson balls didn't bounce as high as the Dunlops. Give me a break.

In school, I received this Chip-like letter from a student who was sent to me for disrupting the quiet of a class meeting: "Dear Mr. Lodish, I'm very, very sorry for interrupting the wonderful quiet in meeting, but I always have an overdose on sugar, as my parents say, and I always get restless in meeting because I'm not good at sitting still. But I'm working at it and cutting down."

3. *Acting irresponsibly by bending the rules.* Tennis is normally played without an umpire or linesman; consequently, players should call balls or infractions only on their side of the net. Yet earlier this week, a player standing on his own baseline questioned a call concerning a ball that landed near my baseline.

At school, I've received all sorts of excuses where students try to make calls on the other side of the net: "Dear Mr. Lodish, I know you probably don't trust me anymore for doing this. But I want you to know that this kind of thing happens every day without notice. I see it. That's sort of the reason I threw food. I didn't know I'd get caught and you probably did these things when you were young. But, hey, let's try to live the rest of the year out. I can guarantee that everything will be okay until then."

4. *Taking frustrations out on others.* I've seen tennis players squeal, scream, groan, and sigh. I've seen players spoil the game by losing their temper, using vile language, throwing their racquet, kicking the ball, or slamming the ball in anger. I've seen others embarrass a weak opponent by being overly gracious or condescending.

In the classroom, I've seen children who, because they couldn't do the work or didn't understand the assignment, bother or make fun of others. I've seen children belittle a classmate because her work was superior to theirs. Students can be ingenious in attempting to excuse bad behavior resulting from frustration. Three fourth graders were sent to me for swearing; five of the boys' parents were lawyers. After

I lectured the boys about how words can hurt and be misinterpreted, Billy (I wouldn't use Nick's real name) asked me, "Do you drive a car?" I responded that I did indeed drive a car. "Do you get angry," Billy asked, "when someone cuts you off?" I again replied that I did. Then Billy pushed in the dagger: "Well, do you ever swear when that happens?" "Honestly," I replied, "sometimes I do." Like a lawyer cross-examining a criminal, Billy pugnaciously inquired, "You're not sent to the principal for swearing. Why should we be?"

I don't mean to sound all negative. Of course, there are also many positive behaviors I see every day on the courts and in the classrooms. I've seen players being scrupulously honest on line calls, keeping in play a ball that might have been out. I've seen players legitimately praising others: "Great hit." "Good overhead." "Nice backhand." Little things, but they add up. Likewise, in my classroom visits, hundreds of times a day I see children praising others, asking for advice, listening intently, sharing with others, cooperating, and working together to make learning a "fun game."

Well, it's approaching the beginning of another school year, and if I'm not working on my slice, serve, backhand, or crosscourt forehand, I'll be at school. But it's still summer vacation and, at least for one more month, my percentages will shift to more time on the courts and less time in my office. I just hope I can remember to wear shorts.

29

If the Shoe Fits:
A Cultural Experience

In July, I began the first of my three cross-cultural Chinese adventures by following directions: "Comfortable walking shoes are essential." I went to three shoe stores, looking in vain for size 6½ tennis shoes to contain my little feet. I finally ended up at the Athlete's Foot in the local mall. I asked the gentleman if he had any size 6½ running shoes. "They don't make adult running shoes in this size," he explained. I asked him what he expected me to do. "Well, if I were you," he replied, "I'd go to China. I bet they have plenty of that size there!" So off I went to China on my search for the perfect size 6½ running shoe. And, as it turned out, to learn a bit of Chinese culture and to develop a new bilingual, intercultural school.

Initially, because I understood the Chinese culture only from the outside in, I made all kinds of faux pas. While buying antiques, I asked the proprietor why gum was stuck on an old rice bowl—it turned out to be the official government seal. Never able to turn down a bargain, I bought a slew of T-shirts for 90 cents apiece that the proprietors, while cautiously looking over their shoulders, hurriedly tried to unload. Later, I read in the *Herald Tribune* in China, "Beijing Prohibits Gloomy T-shirts: The Chinese authorities have abruptly banned the sale of t-shirts with negative messages that were the fashion hit of the summer in Beijing."

While following more serious pursuits in China, I had a chance to visit homes, schools, kindergartens, and day care facilities in factories. In all parts of China, I observed—at least from the outside in—a naturalness and closeness of parents to children (fathers as well as mothers) and many intimate intergenerational moments between grandparents and children.

In two subsequent visits to China, I became part of a consulting team hired to design a bilingual Chinese/English school in a new technology zone in Beijing. Even with severe financial and bureaucratic stumbling blocks, the school has successfully brought together Chinese and English teachers and students in a learning environment of open communication and respect.

Since returning from these extraordinary trips, I have felt compelled to look anew not only at China's culture, but also at our school's culture. Looking from the outside at an unfamiliar school and culture has helped me to see more clearly the forces at work below the surface in our familiar schools and communities.

One such force is the social connectedness—or lack thereof—among the members of a community. In China, I observed several close-knit communities in which adults and kids from many families appeared to know and respect one another. Growing up, I too felt part of a close neighborhood community. Everyone knew everyone. To give you some idea of the closeness of our community, my older brother likes to tell a story from his high school prom of 1959. He was "parking" with his date, Gail, at 6:30 a.m. two blocks from her house when our dad appeared, knocked wildly on the car window, and yelled, "Darn it, Harvey, my golf clubs are in the trunk!"

Unfortunately, as times have changed, many of us don't hang with others—as my brothers and I did—in neighborhoods that are comfortable and secure and where we can socialize easily and get to know one another. The more I hear of the decline in communal spirit within our neighborhoods, the more I've come to believe that schools need to provide an alternative structure for engendering this sense of community, not only for our students and teachers, but also for our parents.

Today, more than ever, I am convinced that without a strong, coherent community, a school will remain at best no more than an adequate place for teaching and learning. With a sense of community, it can become an environment in which caring, respect, and kindness radiate throughout. It can become a place in which honest disagreements are seen as positive forces. It can become a place where we can reweave human connections.

Another intriguing force within our school community, and something I was not able to grasp as an outsider looking in while in China, is the informal network at work in our schools. According to Terrence Deal and Kent Peterson, authors of *The Principal's Role in Shaping School Culture*, there are many "cultural players" in various dramas at all schools. They range from "priests" and "priestesses," old-timers who administer to the needs of the school, to "storytellers" who "personify contemporary exploits through informal history."[5]

But most intriguing to me are their descriptions of "gossips" and "spies" as forces at work in our schools—certainly at work in Chinese schools, as my activities were closely monitored and discussed. "Gossips," according to Deal and Peterson, "keep everyone current on contemporary matters of importance as well as trivia of no special merit . . . and form the informal grapevine that carries information far ahead of formal channels of communication." They describe "spies," "counterspies," and "moles" as important to school culture because they "carry on subterranean negotiations which keep informal checks and balances among various power centers in the school."[6]

In looking at our school from the inside out, it seems that an underlying reason we have carpools, potlucks, parent peer groups, picnics, open houses, and other assorted gatherings may be to provide the "spies," "counterspies," and "moles" with regular updates on the true state of our school, which often are more meaningful than the rational discourse associated with more public events. The so-called "gossips," "spies," and "moles" keep us on our toes and in touch with the real school community.

There is one other intriguing, but lesser known force that tends to hold a community together or pull it apart, be it in China or the United States: a common enemy. I recently attended a 3-day workshop on prejudice reduction. A lot of "isms"—sexism, racism, etc.—were thrashed about, but a new "ism" to me was "leaderism," where members of a community—in our case, teachers, parents, or older kids—occasionally lash out at and test the vulnerability of their leaders. I must say I have been the recipient of this "ism," but all, of course, for the benefit of our community!

Well, I'm sure you're all wondering about my shoes. I went to a number of shoe stores throughout China and Hong Kong. All had many pairs in size 6½, but I just couldn't fit them in my suitcase because it was stuffed with banned Chinese T-shirts and antiques with gum stuck on them.

August

30

Crowds Aren't My Bag

"When we hit that wide open freeway," said Lodish, "I felt like I had been freed; I could breathe again. Crowds aren't my bag."[1]

AUGUST 18, 1969[1]

When the 25th anniversary of the Woodstock Festival was noted a few years back, I was reminiscing with a colleague who teaches a high school course titled "America in the 1960s." I mentioned that I had been to Woodstock many Augusts ago, and that my description of 2 days of unity, love, and mud had been published in the *Cleveland Plain Dealer*.

Sure enough, he had one of his students dig up at the Library of Congress the August 18, 1969 issue. There, on page 9, was the article "Two Heights Men Paint Art Fair as Groovy Fete," containing a picture of my friend and me unloading my VW bus.

I've changed a lot since then. In the 1960s, my Aunt Dorothy labeled me a flower child. Today I can't tell a weed from a flower. (Our science teacher didn't even smirk last summer when I asked her what was wrong with my pepper plants. She simply nodded politely at the three neatly mulched, 6-foot weeds staked to poles in my backyard garden.)

Today I am a conservative principal, that is, a liberal principal with a mortgage. But back in the 1960s, I was a young, rebellious teacher. Here is what *The Real Teachers*, a book of interviews of inner-city teachers, said about me then:

Richard Lodish, 23, stands five foot three, square built, in his suede desert boots. His long blond hair, bushy beard, luxuriant moustache would deter only the more captious among his parents' generation from describing him as "a very nice looking boy."

The book quotes me for posterity:

Teachers should "hip" themselves to the things going around in the community. . . . Yeah, I've always wondered what I would do in a real tight school where the principal comes in your room and says, "You're not teaching reading at ten." I'd probably go berserk.[2]

Yes, indeed, I've changed a lot. In those days, I also used to be a tough guy, a good wrestler. Last summer, at a family get-together, my 14-year-old nephew pinned me in less than 30 seconds while my father, two brothers, and 40 aunts, uncles, cousins, and nephews witnessed my humiliation.

In 25 years, some changes inevitably occur to body and soul. But some Woodstockian thoughts have stayed with me and have helped to define my career as a principal.

1. Crowds still aren't my bag, and the uncrowded, convivial community at our school has helped me, our teachers, and thousands of kids and their parents to feel at home.
2. Weed children—and other assorted varieties—receive the same respect as flower children. They are all allowed to grow and flourish, with healthy nutrients spread and sprinkled by their teachers.
3. Although a good education requires hard work and intellectual rigor, there is still room for "groovy fetes." Warm fuzzies, pet shows, worm farms, and butterfly dances all have their place.
4. It's okay to be a rebel of sorts, to voice strongly one's own convictions and go against the grain. This holds true for children as well as teachers—and even occasionally for the principal. In fact, I often hire teachers who have a bit of rebelliousness about them; it makes for a richer, fuller,

more interesting—if more difficult to handle—teaching community.

5. It's all right for children to lose, even to be embarrassed, as long as teachers help them to handle the loss and the loss of face with sensitivity and kindness, and to learn from these mistakes and bad experiences. (It does help, though, not to have one's relatives around.)

Finally, I have carried with me from my Woodstock days this thought: Although teachers of young children must anticipate the rigors and rituals of the next stages of schooling, they need to help children live in and enjoy the present—or to use a Woodstock era phrase, "Be here now."

I guess I still agree with some of that flower child stuff. Unless, of course, there are too many people being here now. Hey, man, you know, "crowds aren't my bag."

31

Too Many Choices

You have brains in your head.
You have feet in your shoes.
You can steer yourself
Any direction you choose.

DR. SEUSS[3]

This must be the decade—or at least the year—of choice. It seems everywhere we turn, from the marketplace to education to parenting, there are just too many choices. We've always had choices, but today we are in danger of being overwhelmed by them.

These thoughts about choice began when my daughter came home for summer vacation and cut up my Levi's for shorts. (She wanted these Levi shorts to fit over my boxer shorts, which she also took back to college with her.) My 20-year-old Levi's had finally died anyway, and they didn't fit over my waist, let alone my thighs. So off I went to a Levi's store in Georgetown, where I naively asked for "a pair of Levi's." The salesclerk began reciting a litany of choices that sounded like a freshman's college catalog. "There are the original button-fly Levi's 501s with the straight leg; 505s with a regular fit, straight leg; 512s, slim fit, narrow leg opening; 517s, traditional fit, boot cut; 517s, relaxed fit, boot cut; 550s, relaxed fit, tapered leg; 560s, tapered leg, loose fit; 580s, baggy fit, single pleat; Levi's Signatures 540s, relaxed fit, straight leg; 545s, loose fit, slightly tapered leg; 546s, loose fit, single pleat, slightly tapered leg; 44530s, Lean Jeans (sounds like diet Levi's made by the Healthy Choice company); and 44552s, relaxed, designed with a curved seat for optimum comfort." Many come in a choice of regular wash, prewash, and stonewash.

Bewildered by the choices presented, I tried on a few pairs of jeans and got stuck trying to unbutton the button fly on the original 501s. I'm not sure what cowboys who wore 501s in the Wild West did to put out fires, but it would have taken me until the embers died down. Robert D. Haas, Chairman and Chief Executive Officer of Levi Strauss & Company, assured me that "having grown up with 501s [he] developed some dexterity with button flys," although he understood my "preference for a zipper."

Choice in the 1990s has become the intentional mantra for education and an unintentional quandary for parents and kids. Since the publication of *Education by Choice* by John Coons and Steven Sugarman in 1978,[4] there has been a parade of programs, proposals, policies, and prescriptions relating to choice in our schools. Everything from vouchers to privatization to magnet schools to charter schools to state academies has been debated or tried. I think the issue of diversity in educational endeavors is crucial, and that different schools should have different goals and define them and act on them. But as I discovered in the Levi's store, choices can confuse and mislead us. Choice alone, even if presented in a form both perspicuous and credible to families, will not lead to better results. More than anything else, good schools, in whatever forms, need excellent teachers and involved parents. Choice may improve the latter, but will not necessarily bring about the former.

Parents are beset not only by confusion on school choices but also by parenting choices. There are hundreds of books on parenting in any bookstore, from *Why Johnny Can't Concentrate* to *The Emotional Problems of Normal Children*, and there are now some 97 parenting magazines. David Elkind, professor at Tufts University, says that many parents are choosing to parent by technique, rather than by intuition,[5] how-to books may be replacing family traditions and intergenerational and community support systems.

Parents have to make all kinds of choices today that weren't available when Dr. Spock was alone on the bookshelf. The most pressing questions include: How shall we choose to divide our time between family, community, and the job? How will these choices affect the kids? What constitutes a family? I, for one, resist telling parents how to parent (Lord knows I have enough of my own challenges in that area). It is clear to me and to most "experts," however, that there is no substitute for parents spending quality *and* quantity time with their kids, and that finding more family time may require sacrificing professional responsibilities. As someone said, "The problems we have are not from overwork, but from underbeing."

And then there are the choices we offer kids. Some kids, even young ones, have the maturity to make decisions; others need clear directions and limits. Excellent teachers (those who should be free to make choices) know how to loosen the reins for those who can handle options and limit choices for those who require more stability and structure.

As children get older and leave the cocoon of elementary school, they begin—as they should—to take responsibility for making their own choices. The freedom to choose, however, can be perplexing for kids. The airwaves saturate our youngsters with choices, good and bad, while marketing professionals plot ways to entice our youngsters to choose an event, a product, an activity, or a style. Even as children-centered van services transport privileged youngsters to their destinations of choice, too many of our nation's children face an array of terrifying choices on the streets of our cities. Children should be able to trust adults, and adults must provide clear, consistent support and guidance to help them negotiate what has become increasingly a minefield of choices.

Although we may not be able to—or want to—go back to fewer, simpler choices, more than ever we need to make informed choices that sustain core values of family, community, integrity, and hard work. We need choices that enrich us and others, that push and prod us to imagine and to dream, that engage and excite us in learning; choices that enable us to show compassion toward others and that fit with who we are and what we want to become as an educated nation, as parents, as teachers, and as children.

I'm certainly comfortable with the choice I made. After spending an hour and a half at the Levi's store, I finally chose the 517s relaxed fit with a big seat. With my terrible hand-eye coordination, it's a good thing I didn't choose the original 501s with the button fly.

32

The Last Transition

Summer vacation is just about over, and I have finally succumbed to my mother's ways. *Kein Ein Hora pu pu pu.* I heard this saying a thousand times while growing up as my mother would end each description of the good that had just transpired. "Mrs. Hazelett called to say that Richard would go on to fourth grade. *Kein Ein Hora pu pu pu.*" "Richard came back from Woodstock in one piece. *Kein Ein Hora pu pu pu.*" "My son finally practiced lunchroom manners. *Kein Ein Hora pu pu pu.*" "My child in the principal's office wore his bifocals, kept his tennis shorts on, buttoned his Levi's, and tied his tiny 6½ shoes all by himself. *Kein Ein Hora pu pu pu.*" Loosely translated, from generations in Kiev, Russia: "It should continue to be good without someone casting an evil eye."

Our students will soon be back at school, transitioning ever so slowly from childhood to adulthood. *Kein Ein Hora pu pu pu.* And we adults think we can predict many of the transitions they will go through from childhood to adulthood.

We can predict that they will grow bigger and taller and smarter, or as skeptic Judith Viorst said, we can predict that someday these "blobs of passionate protoplasm" will finally get well, after they emerge from a long disease with an awesome list of symptoms called childhood.[6]

Yes, I guess we grownups can predict with some accuracy something about each child. But the real thrill and scary part of being a teacher or a parent or a principal is being proven wrong in our predictions.

And I imagine that many of our children are also starting to think about their own transitions and are beginning to label themselves—"I'm good at this, bad at that." Growing up does mean narrowing the distance between dreams and possibilities.

But if I have one plea for our children, it is this: They shouldn't limit their possibilities. They shouldn't be too hard on themselves. They should not classify themselves too early. They can choose to change. "This freedom to choose," Viorst writes, "is the burden and the gift we receive when we leave childhood."[7]

The secret, as I see it, is to make the transition to adulthood without losing the child within. Like two of my heroes—Danny Kaye, the great entertainer and comedian, and Maurice Sendak, the writer of children's books—we need to keep an intense nostalgia for childhood, a passionate affiliation with childhood. We need to find the child in us, seek it out, and set it free.

Our children must also remember that people of all ages are going through transitions in life. They need to remember that many grownups, including teachers, parents, and principals, are coming full circle in their transitions.

As our children are working themselves away from depending on adults, many men and women of the older generation will someday become dependent on them, and these older people will want to touch those who will be there when they are gone—the last transition.

The last transition came home to me with the passing of my mother, who was a third-grade teacher for 34 years and a child at heart. I think she would have wanted me to share the last words she spoke—or rather, sang.

My brothers and I had been sitting with my mom during her final days. Full of painkillers and drifting in and out of consciousness, my mom was unable to talk. To pass the time, my brothers and I sang silly songs from our childhood. Suddenly, in the midst of "Be-Bop-A-Lula," from somewhere deep in her soul, my mother started to sing along with us.

As we sang "Be-Bop-A-Lula," she responded, "She's my baby." When we continued with "Be-Bop-A-Lula," she added, "I don't mean maybe." And on it went for an incredible and touching 5 minutes.

You have to envision how strange, how miraculous, how child-like it was for a bald 72-year-old grandmother, weighing 86 pounds, to sing this old rock 'n' roll song. But that's how I like to remember my mom—in her last transition, as a child again.

And I'm sure that's how she remembers me—her child in the principal's office. *Kein Ein Hora pu pu pu.*

The
End

References

Foreword

1. Whitehead, A. N. (1949). *The aims of education* (p.13). New York: Mentor.

Introduction

1. McCormick, P. (1994, January 6). Laughing it up: *Washington Post*, p. C-5.
2. Ibid.
3. Shogren, E. (1993, March 17). Teaching lessons in living. *Los Angeles Times*, p. A-1.
4. Boyer, E. (1991, April 15). *Role of the Quaker school in today's society.* Speech given at the George School, Newtown, PA.
5. Sha, R. K. (1990, July 31). Literary detective on the trail of memory: Why Dennis McFarland gave up the piano for the world of words. *Washington Post*, p. D-1.

September

1. Heymont, G. (1987, January). Maurice Sendak plays second fiddle. *Amtrak Express*, p. 32.
2. Digilio, A. (1985, November 17). Talent search: Aptitude testing for principals. *Washington Post Education Review*, p. 8.

3. Raebeck, B. (1994, June). The school as a humane business. *Phi Delta Kappan*, pp. 761-765.
4. Deal, T., & Peterson, K. (1994). *The leadership paradox: Balancing logic and artistry in schools*. San Francisco: Jossey-Bass.

October

1. Kaufman, J. (1989, June 26). Happy birthday, Prince Charming. *People Weekly*, p. 30.
2. Dahl, R. (1988). *Matilda* (pp. 7-8). New York: Penguin.

November

1. Maclean, N. (1976). *A river runs through it* (p. 8). Chicago: University of Chicago Press.
2. Kohn, A. (1990). *The brighter side of human nature: Altruism and empathy in everyday life*. New York: Basic Books.
3. Kohn, A. (1991, March). Caring kids: The role of the schools. *Phi Delta Kappan*, p. 499.
4. Trillin, C. (1994, June 20). Messages from my father. *The New Yorker*, p. 64.
5. Himes, G. (1994, July 29). Havens: Peace, love and lawsuit. *Washington Post*, Weekend, p. 12.
6. Clem, S. (1994, Spring). Educating the heart: The moral life of schools. *NAIS Academic Forum*, p. 1.

December

1. Bolt, R. (1960). *A man for all seasons* (pp. 8, 9). New York: Vintage International.
2. Burton, V. L. (1939). *Mike Mulligan and his steam shovel*. Boston: Houghton Mifflin.
3. LaMotte, A. K. (1988, November). Penn Charter's traveling minstrels. *Friends Journal*, pp. 12-15.
4. Sugarman, C. (1991, August 13). Shaving a few pounds: Lying about weight. *Washington Post*, Health, p. 16.

5. Tomlinson, T. M., & Cross, C. (1991, September). Student effort: The key to higher standards. *Educational Leadership*, p. 70.
6. Krucoff, C. (1984, February 11). Quoted in: Mind over manners: Starting young with the empress of etiquette. *Washington Post*, Section G, p. 1.

January

1. Jones, M., Jr. (1990, December 3). Quoted in: Bring back the monsters. *Newsweek*, p. 64.
2. Beard, H., & McKie, R. (1988). *A dictionary of silly words about growing up*. New York: Workman.
3. Erikson, E. H. (1950). *Childhood and society* (Chap. 7). New York: Norton.
4. Levine, S. (1989). *Promoting adult growth in schools: The promise of professional development*. Boston: Allyn & Bacon.
5. Levine, S. L. (1989, January). The principal as adult developer. *Principal*, p. 17.
6. Angelou, M. (1990). Human family. In *I shall not be moved* (pp. 4-5). New York: Random House.
7. Ibid.

February

1. Johnson, E. (1970). *Teaching school points picked up* (p. vii). Boston: National Association of Independent Schools.
2. Ricciotti, J. A. (1988, March). Good teaching: The goose bump response. *Principal*, p. 41.
3. Ibid.
4. Kantrowitz, B., & Wingert, P. (1989, April 17). How kids learn. *Newsweek*, p. 56.
5. Bruner, J. (1977). *The process of education*. Cambridge, MA: Harvard University Press.
6. Ashton-Warner, S. (1963). *Teacher* (p. 93). New York: Simon and Schuster.

A CHILD IN THE PRINCIPAL'S OFFICE

March

1. Montagu, A. (1981). *Growing young.* New York: McGraw-Hill.

April

1. Goodman, J. (1992). *Elementary schooling for critical democracy* (pp. 109, 118). Albany: State University of New York Press.
2. Hyde, N. (1989, July 11). The security jacket: A Washington habit, no matter how hot. *Washington Post,* Style, p. 1.
3. Edelman, M. W. (1992, June 5). Graduation speech given at Sidwell Friends School, Washington, DC.
4. Sternberg, R. J. (1994, November). Allowing for thinking styles. *Educational Leadership,* pp. 36-40.
5. Ibid., p. 38.

May

1. Westbrook, R. B. (1993). *John Dewey and American democracy* (p. 169). Ithaca, NY: Cornell University Press.
2. Gardner, H. (1991). *The unschooled mind: How children think and how schools should teach* (p. 110). New York: Basic Books.
3. Ibid.
4. Heide, F. P. (1971). *The shrinking of Treehorn.* New York: Holiday House.
5. de Saint-Exupéry, A. (1943). *The little prince* (p. 87). San Diego, CA: Harcourt Brace Jovanovich.

June

1. Gorman, C. (1992, January 20). Sizing up the sexes. *Time,* p. 45.
2. Carlos, A. (1992, January 21). Desk jockeys to teach. *Montgomery Journal,* p. 1.
3. Holt, J. (1978). *Never too late.* Boston: Delacorte/Seymour Lawrence.
4. Grogan, D. (1991, December 2). School of soft knocks. *People Weekly,* p. 72.
5. Rosenfeld, M. (1991, December 15). Spielberg in Neverland. *Washington Post,* p. G-4.

July

1. Tolstoy, L. (1967). *Tolstoy on education* (p. 227). Chicago: University of Chicago Press.
2. Capital comment. (1986, June). *Washingtonian*, p. 21.
3. Letters. (1986, August). *Washingtonian*, pp. 32-33.
4. U.S. Tennis Association. (1992). *Friend at court* (p. 117). New York: Author.
5. Deal, T. E., & Peterson, K. P. (1990). *The principal's role in shaping school culture* (p. 17). Washington, DC: Government Printing Office.
6. Ibid., p. 18.

August

1. Hatch, S. (1969, August 18). Two Heights men paint art fair as groovy fete. *Cleveland Plain Dealer*, p. 9.
2. Sterling, P. (Ed.). (1972). *The real teachers* (p. 117). New York: Vintage.
3. Seuss, Dr. (1990). *Oh, the places you'll go!* (p. 2). New York: Random House.
4. Coons, J. E., & Sugarman, S. D. (1978). *Education by choice*. Berkeley: University of California Press.
5. Sessions, L. (1994, October 18). Focus on parenting: The how-to market aimed at moms and dads. *Washington Post*, p. B-5.
6. Viorst, J. (1987). *Necessary losses* (p. 145). New York: Fawcett.
7. Ibid., p. 158.

CORWIN
PRESS

The **Corwin Press logo**—a raven striding across an open book—represents the happy union of courage and learning. We are a professional-level publisher of books and journals for K–12 educators, and we are committed to creating and providing resources that embody these qualities. Corwin's motto is "Success for All Learners."